Listening to Grace
unlearning insights and poems

To Amy,
Here's to listening
to Grace and all
the blessings that
abound!
Sandy Wilder

Sanford C. Wilder

Educare Unlearning Institute
711B Wind Rivers
Grafton, IL 62037

ISBN: 978-0-615-82484-0

Contents

Foreword

This is one of the most profound, precious, peace-instilling books I have ever read. It is also challenging, but in a gentle and at the same time quietly insistent way, prodding the reader to ease or work out of her or his comfort zones.

Some years ago, my life which had moved forward for so many years in an apparently smooth and successful manner, in a space of a few months, suddenly came crashing down: marriage, work, finances, health and especially what I believed was the ultimate spiritual path, fell to pieces.

In the midst of all this turmoil, a friend sent me a quotation from a center I had never heard of called the Educare Unlearning Institute, in Grafton, Illinois. I decided to subscribe to the free Unlearning Insights sent daily, 365 days a year, by its founder, Sandy Wilder.

I started awaiting them impatiently. They were so special, so utterly different from anything I had ever read before, both in style, tone and content. They rapidly became a real lifeline for me – and still are a major reference point in my life.

Then, a year later, I had the unique privilege of taking a workshop at the Institute. This turned out to be the most remarkable training I ever had in an existence of constant learning (not to mention running my own workshops for 20 years). In the first half day, Sandy created a space of unconditional love and complete non-judgment, which lasted the whole six-day workshop.

This book, written in the author's unique style, will open unto you broad new vistas you never dreamed existed. It reflects all the qualities present in his workshops. Sandy writes with a unique combination of immense kindness and complete trust in the reader's fundamental goodness and ability to understand.

He also constantly prods us to let go of the comfortable past and venture trustingly into the unknown – a challenging assignment for all those who are control freaks (and there are many in our culture!) His unrelenting call to live authentically and listen deeply to our heart, is the foundation of any meaningful life.

He dared me to look at my shadow side, something I had vigorously denied existed during my former spiritual path, claiming that it was "unreal." But brushing the dust under the carpet is not the best way of eliminating it! Sandy is still helping me "uncover and unlearn some of the beliefs and corresponding behaviors" that were keeping me "locked in unprogressive habits, cycles and patterns."

At the same time, he constantly reminds us that, in the vaster plan of things, all is well, and that we all have a personal G.P.S. (God Positioning System – if I may dare the expression) that will ultimately guide us all home.

One of the richest insights you may well gain from this book is the vital understanding that because we are all linked through the infinite Love that holds us all together, every step we take toward awakening ourselves is an awakening step for all mankind.

This is a book to read daily, and, especially because of its universal, non-denominational nature, a book to offer to anyone and everyone.

Byron Katie, a leader in the field of personal development, has stated that the world's number one problem is confusion. I am convinced that this book's divine simplicity and clarity will appeal to all.

Pierre Pradervand
Author, The Gentle Art of Blessing
Geneva, Switzerland 2013

Preface

As much as my name is under the title as author of this book, that feels like a misnomer. I merely listen each day for the message I'm being asked to share, and then take the dictation.

Listening to Grace is synonymous to me with listening to the Inner Teacher, the "still, small voice," the divine influence within the heart, that which speaks to each of us and takes form as our authentic voices.

These are selections from daily unlearning insights and poems over the past three years that I send to anyone interested. A few poems are also included that were written earlier. They are arranged thematically, but I'm sure you will find lots of overlap across chapters. The book can be read straight through, beginning with any chapter, or just opened randomly to an unlearning insight or poem.

The word "unlearning" is used because I am starting from the premise that each of us has within us a hidden wholeness. We are the full consciousness of the Divine, but for various reasons have forgotten our sacred heritage and infinite potential.

We have been conditioned and instructed away from Oneness into a delusion of separateness and isolation. So, we get to unlearn (i.e. recognize and release), that which we are not, so that which we are shines forth with radiant brightness, clarity, freedom and love.

Everything in this book rings true in my heart and experience. Abstract metaphysical concepts, were not revealed by Grace, and therefore are not included.

I offer these as simple moments of clarity during this period in my journey. I hope they may resonate with you, so that together we may see the impersonal nature of the aberration of separation, and the universal oneness of Life. As we allow our limited sense of self to diminish, we experience the inside-out embrace of transformation, and suffering begins to recede.

I have no interest in telling people what to believe. I am committed to helping those interested find what they believe in their hearts, and dance this out with authenticity and passion, while surrendering everything to Grace!

As you are reading, resist the temptation to ask yourself, "What did he mean by this?" Rather ask Grace, "What do I need to see right now?"

Thank you for being open to awakening to your authentic Self: the gift waiting within, for each of us.

Sandy Wilder
July 2013

Unlearning Insights and Poems

Chapter 1

Authenticity
Reveals Freedom

There is no more time for anything but living from your deepest truth every moment! This is authenticity. Why consciously do otherwise?

When you find your authentic Self, you experience the freedom of standing defenseless in front of another because you see and feel only love.

This summer I took myself on a solo stillness walk on the Maine coast, and sat down for half a day to appreciate the matchless beauty around me, and just listen. What came up for me were two questions, and an irresistible urge to live into the answers. Here are the questions:

- What's the point of life for me right now?
- What is really important?

If my answers to those questions are clear, which they are, then the only conceivable response is to be 100% devoted to living from that clarity. Am I waiting for some distant magical thing to happen and then I will go for it? Come on!

When I hear and feel the music, can I do anything but give myself completely to the dance?

When you want to grow something in a garden, one of the first things you do is provide a space for it. You clear out what is not needed and prepare the soil to receive the new seeds.

What kind of space do you create for your own growth? Is it large and deep enough for what you are hoping to grow?

Have you cleared out what is not needed? Have you ventured below the surface to see what might be growing there undetected, which might strangle the new birth?

Many of us want transformation, but we are only allowing the surface space in our lives for maintaining our current status quo. Is this the time to see if the space you are providing for new growth is the one that Grace is calling forth? Do some priorities need to shift?

When you are not attached to defending anything, including your self-image, you are no longer afraid of being verbally attacked or devalued. Your identity can't be touched because it eternally exists beyond reproach.

Some questions to consider if you are interested in awakening to the radiant freedom that is you.

- Do you recognize authenticity when you experience it? How would you describe it?
- How about inauthenticity? How would you describe it?
- Which would you rather interact with? (Your answer may be obvious, but deeply contemplate why.)
- Here's the zinger: Which of the two words better describes you: authentic or inauthentic?
- If the recipe for becoming more authentic means being more vulnerable, are you willing? (Vulnerable means being willing to look at your shadow side, and uncover and unlearn some of the beliefs and corresponding behaviors that are keeping you locked in unprogressive habits, cycles, and patterns.)
- Are you willing to admit you don't have all the answers?
- Are you willing to really listen?
- Are you open to an unconditioned relationship with the Divine where you don't lead?

Really sit in stillness with these questions. Listen honestly to your heart. It won't lie.

What would your experience be like if you said "No thanks" when it comes to your consciousness to dwell in:

- regretting the past,
- predicting the future, or
- battling in the present?

In the last five years I have felt deeply called to find and express my innate divine authenticity. In addition to living in the questions on the opposite page, it has involved two main functions:

1. Answering this question: What do I really want in life? (And daily acting and prioritizing as if I mean it!)
2. Identifying and running <u>at</u> the darkness (the scary shadows) vs. running <u>from</u> the darkness (at which I excelled).

What has this meant for me?

With Grace as my Guide, I have never felt so alive, free, and connected: so at one with Life, as I do today.

Find Your Self on Fire!

Each of us has a bonfire
that is kindling deep within.
It is forever fueled
by the same non-consuming Source
that burned the bush.
It is speaking to us, as well.

We are here together,
in this fiery furnace of Grace,
To fan the part of us that is glowing
To listen for the message in another's crackle
To blow on each other's embers
To feel Love's warmth permeating our surface tension
To let the sparks fly!

You are invited to "consider the lilies,"
to share the white light
of Truth's clarity,
where our souls burn together
as logs set ablaze in authenticity and divine sweetness.

May we surrender in this sacred hearth
to Love's fire,
where we find our purified voice,
and rediscover
our innate innocence, freedom and calling.

We are needed on fire!

When you are living from the one authentic Self, your innate Oneness, a beauty and simplicity emerges. You lose interest in being right, or better than anyone. Your desire for others to act according to your plan has been blown away by the winds of Grace.

Someone comes up to you. You check in with your heart, and listen, and speak, or not. If someone agrees, great! If someone disagrees, great!

You exude reliability. You are reliably you. Not necessarily what everyone (or anyone) wants you to be. You are honest, genuine: acting from your center in Grace.

To develop your authentic capacity, notice your thoughts, feelings, beliefs, stories, word choices, actions, etc.

Notice what feels real and true: that which resonates and creates harmonics of your song.

Notice what feels fake and whorish: where you set aside your integrity, your inner peace, in order to get something you want (like the appreciation of another). Notice when you do this, and how what you get is never really enough. Experience how hollow and fake it feels to be inauthentic.

When you taste your authentic Self, it ignites a hunger and thirst that will never be quenched in any other way. You are at home in your sweet spot. Finally.

When you begin to live authentically, a lot of things that drove you start transforming. You lose interest in how hard something may be, or wishing it was easy. The desire to create an ideal future is yielding to being in awe of now, no matter where you are.

The attraction to leaving a legacy is evaporating because your only wish is that people see and feel their own divine radiance. The need to incessantly control your environment, is eclipsed by surrendering everything to Grace.

It's becoming less about trying to make a difference, and more about being your authentic Self. It's not that you don't care about change, it's that you just care. Full time. The impact of your caring is not up to you.

Kinda simple, really.

There is an unmistakable sense of your authentic Self that can be experienced here and now. It is awakened to, and revealed by, Grace.

It is not just another idea that tumbles through the mind. It is not a concept that has been memorized from a sacred text. It is not an emotional feeling like happiness, which comes and goes. It is not a personality with a bundle of preferences. It does not require anything to maintain it. It needs no defending.

You experience your authentic Self while you are in your body, but there is no sense of being distracted by your body. You feel unshakably real, and transcend, yet unite, the duplicity of two opposite worlds: the material and spiritual.

You are indestructible and flowing forth without self-conscious concerns. You exist beyond fatigue or diminishment. You move in an effortless dance. You feel and witness divinely ordered improvisation where truth, humor, silence, and graceful perspicacity flow unobstructed.

You feel a groundedness that is anchored to a timeless now. Your words are formed for you and flow through you. Your heart is compassionately connected to all hearts. You are need-free because everything required is available and present. You are the felt presence of immovable Love.

One

One.
Not two.

Being.
Not beings.

Life.
Not lives.

I AM.
Not I was.

Are you able to be vulnerable with others? If not, what are you protecting?

Today a deep splinter of conditioned unconsciousness became conscious and was thus removed. It had only been buried as long as I have conscious memory.

This afternoon I realized how I had been assigning an underlying enigmatic fear and pain to others. I had believed that if I am judged and verbally attacked, then the individuals saw nothing worth loving in me.

What surfaced today through deep meditative inquiry and quiet listening was, I was living in a story that said: "If they saw nothing worth loving in me, then I believed they were right. I have no worth." Believing this I felt an unbearable pain, and so in my story, I blamed them.

Today's dawning grace was that my pain was because I had given away my sense of my worth.

They had not taken it. Worth can't be stolen from us. It is innate. I had believed that how someone treats me was a statement about my worth. Wow.

How someone treats me is a statement about how they treat me. Period. It cannot impact my worth.

Now, next time I am judged and verbally attacked, I will listen as they tell me about their beliefs. I am open to learning from what they are saying. But nothing they can say or do can change my inviolate worth.

Hard to put into words how huge this is for me. I have been trying to remove this splinter for the last 40 years, ever since I was introduced to spirituality. Thank you Grace.

When you are on a walk and you come upon a flower, it gives you all of itself by simply being what it is. It does not need you to notice it, for it to grow. Nor is it depleted or fatigued in any way by this giving.

You receive the gift of the flower as you appreciate the reality of its beauty, as an expression of Nature. If you pause long enough to breathe in this sacred moment, you may feel refreshed and inspired.

You too, are Nature's flower, gently radiating the simplicity of your authentic Self, wherever you are planted. You are enough.

One day when our daughter was in high school, she turned to me and said:

"If you and Mom weren't my parents, I would still be me, but I wouldn't look like this."

Think about it.

You are not a self-conscious being that is forever encased in endless thoughts about yourself. That "person" that you keep returning to is what you have been conditioned by society to believe is you. Where does that self-centered magnetic noun go when you are in your zone?

Picture yourself completely involved in an activity (e.g. watching a sunset, playing a sport, dancing full out, doing whatever you LOVE to do…). We have all experienced these moments, as a child, and throughout life.

These reveal an unselfed-self: one that has no self-consciousness, and is literally a verb in full expression. You are the watching not the watcher, the playing not the player, the dancing not the dancer, the doing not the doer, the loving not the lover…

Don't let the needy, black hole noun, reign over the divinely natural, blossoming verb, you forever are.

Whenever you believe you are separate from others, you are not coming from your divinely authentic Self. This may manifest as the desire to control. You may feel you need to do something so that a situation is "connected" the way you think it should be.

Here are some examples:

- This project is not going the way I think it should, so I need to take over and make it happen.
- This child should not behave this way, so I need to control him so he will act accordingly and I will get the results I want.
- I need to make sure my friend has the right ideas so that she doesn't have to suffer, therefore I will tell her what she needs to know.

You are inadvertently communicating: "I, the superior, need to direct them, the inferior, so that my sense of harmony is restored (for the greater good, of course)."

Alternatively, when you are coming from your divinely authentic Self, you know you are connected to others. You naturally trust there is one, shared Intelligence that is governing everything and everyone.

Your actions will reflect a sense of mutual respect, accepting that each person (regardless of age or stage) is as tapped into the divine as you are. You may find yourself addressing situations from the standpoint of listening and discovering together, yielding your will to the yet-to-be-revealed order of the moment.

You are communicating, "I honor the Divinity in us all, and am openly watching it unfold life."

Which approach would you rather be around?

Have you ever tried to please others by acting in a way that will not bother them? On the outside this may not look like such a bad idea, because it "keeps the peace in the family." The problem is that this can become a full time job, in which your authentic Self is buried and your egoic self is running the show.

As this gets old, resentment starts to build towards those you are constantly trying to please. Since this does not feel good, you may start to distance yourself from them. Although you want to be who you are, and fulfill your creative potential in life, you mistakenly think you can't do this around these people.

The issue is not the people. You have trained them to expect certain behaviors from you by your lack of authenticity. The only way out of this cycle of atrophy is to recognize that it is slowly killing you, and destroying any intimacy in your life.

Ask yourself: What do I really want in life? What is my deepest yearning? These may not be easy questions, but your answers can help you begin to speak and act from your authentic Self, and find a new center from which to live. This will ultimately be the biggest gift you could ever give yourself, and others.

When you are living in Yes, you can say "No" to another without being concerned if they will be disappointed. Their response is simply their response. Period. Your authentic "Yes" or "No" encourages them to live in their Yes, (even if they don't know it at the time).

This isn't being insensitive. Nobody wins when you hide from living and speaking what is authentically true in your heart.

When you say "Yes" to your authentic Self, your entire world becomes a "Yes!" When you say "No" to your authentic Self, you will exhaust yourself looking everywhere for love, finding it ever-fleeting, and never enough to fill your void. Been there, done that.

When you love someone enough to release them from needing to act a certain way to make you happy, you give them a huge vote for being their authentic Self. What a precious gift!

When you love yourself enough to release yourself from needing to act a certain way to make others happy, you give yourself a huge vote for being your authentic Self. Another precious gift!

Here's to voting for authenticity.

If someone inspires you, the focus is not to memorize their words, or imitate their actions. This is hollow. The key is to discover and develop your unique connection with the same unrestricted Love they are expressing.

When you allow your heart to open to your authentic expression of Soul, give yourself completely to it. Don't hold anything back. Let your entire life be choreographed by Grace.

When unlearning, you are never being asked to give up anything of authentic value. You are being invited into a space where you get to look at your self-concept, and realize what you are attached to for your happiness, peace, success, and sense of worth.

It could be a title, an award, an accomplishment, a relationship, a possession, really anything that makes you think because of this you are special. You don't have to give them up, just realize that they don't define you.

Without any of these you are absolutely extraordinary, because you are the individual consciousness of the Divine... and so is every he and she in the universe. Unlearning removes the basis for comparison, and delivers Oneness.

Are you in relationship with others in a way that encourages them to value their authentic truth?

Are you in relationship with *yourself* in a way that encourages you to value *your* authentic truth?

Please do not answer these too quickly. Listen to your heart's genuine response...

Authenticity Reveals Freedom

Chapter 2

Listening to Grace

The activity of grace is the way that Love reaches us here and now. When it is wholeheartedly invited, it lands and takes over the reins of whatever it is you are under the illusion you are controlling in that moment.

If you are not willing to let go, Grace just waits, maintaining your wholeness, while you are convicted around manipulating your current deficiency. You may even wonder, with all your praying, why aren't you getting the results you think you should? (That would be control.)

Grace asks you to open wide, and surrender everything, and everyone (including yourself and all your desires), to its natural order.

Listening to Grace

Setting aside the space
Hooking the chrysalis on the tree of Grace
Climbing into the blank page
Following no routine
No repeating paths
Always new, always now
Ever green, alive
Opening
Listening
Willing to suspend judgment
No where to go
Seeing how Grace reveals itself today

The mind doubts the birth
The heart mutes the mind
Stillness, listening
The dictation begins
As listening and writing merge
Ideas appear
Some stay, some go
No holding on to anything
They place themselves
Today's offering starts to pulse
Reforming itself
Into what is called forth now

Opening, wider
Stillness, listening
Becoming flows into being
Staying in the chrysalis until
It's time to take flight
Off it goes on wings of gratitude
Where it lands is up to Grace

One definition of grace is: the imparting of unconditional Divine blessings. When we are inspired by grace, we find ourselves naturally giving and receiving these kinds of blessings. This reinforces the immeasurable Oneness of all Being.

When we allow the ego to steer us, instead of freely bestowing unconditional blessings, we impart calculated, conditional, withholdings with each other. This reinforces our belief in scarcity, limitation, separation, isolation, and a multiplicity of beings.

If we as individuals aren't allowing ourselves to be driven by grace to live in this way, what's the point? Really.

God's
Relentless
Affection
Celebrating
Everyone (no matter what you or they have done, ever)

G race does not change us, it reveals us.

E ach of us has within us an indissoluble, direct communication link with the Divine. It is built in.

When we are first learning to consciously listen to this Inner Teacher, it is common to hear static: mindless chatter, story-filled drama, judgments, etc. J. B. Phillips in his book *The Ring of Truth*, calls it "diabolical interference." I call it mildly interesting noise. It is just egoic echoes.

Let it play itself out. Don't fight it. Just notice that it is there. It will fade. Don't feed it with frustration or disappointment. It's just a cloud that will move by or evaporate. There is nothing wrong with you because a cloud is present. You are not the cloud. You are not the mind that is making the noise.

You have the conscious clarity to recognize what is you, and what is not. This is a HUGE first step.

G race is our experience of the activity of Oneness.

I f our focus in prayer is to figure out the next statement of truth to help and heal us, then we may frequently be in search of that evasive perfect concept to act as our silver bullet.

If this is the conditioning we are acting out, then we may find we go through quick-lived highs and extended lows as a continual seeker of truthful concepts. This can turn into an intellectual pursuit that feels hollow and disconnected from God and others.

If instead our focus is to listen, by being open and receptive to what Love is always imparting to us, we will find we are united with the divine in a forever-deepening exploration of experiential oneness.

Here there is a constant feeling into, and surrendering to, Grace, for everything, not just when we need extra help. Our heart is permeated with such an illuminating presence of authentic Reality, that we feel embraced, expanded, and guided moment-by-moment, completely connected to all life as one infinite community.

Grace is not earned by being good, or lost by being bad, like a Santa Claus list. God doesn't keep a list. Grace arrives when you are ready to be transformed by it, even if you think you are not...

When you have total trust in Grace you don't try to sustain anything. What would be the point?

You are no longer steering your (or anyone else's) ship.

You are not responsible for what enters your life. To try to control what happens to you is an endless, exhausting run on the hamster wheel. You feel very much like your life is "out of control."

Doing this will impact all your relationships, repelling the people around you. (The authentic ones will let you know this.)

What you are responsible for is what you believe about what enters your life: the stories you create (or not). This is your business.

To the degree you take your stories to Truth, questioning their validity, you will feel very much like your life is "under control:" Grace's control, nor yours.

As you surrender your cherished stories and desires to Grace, people find themselves feeling good around you. They are naturally able to say things to you that they can't say to others, because you don't judge them, you listen. It is not all about you and your way.

As you allow Grace to run your own life, it gives everyone a vote of confidence that they can do the same. What a simple, priceless gift.

The main challenge I hear from people in relation to listening to God, once they get past all the noise, is that they don't hear anything.

Really? Nothing? How long have you listened? 5 seconds, 10, maybe 20?

What do you do when you don't hear anything? (Figure you aren't good at this? Or, God isn't good at this? Or, go do something you are good at that is not so challenging?)

Here are some options for why you may not hear anything:

- Could it be that what God is saying is, "Be still and appreciate the deep, alive, beauty of silence."
- Could it be that you are being led to feel into the presence of this burgeoning moment of Life?
- Could it be that you are listening with your head instead of your heart?
- Could it be that the question you asked God was a closed-ended question (like either this or that) and you were not open to, or could not recognize, a 3rd option?
- Could it be that you don't recognize the communication because it doesn't fit within the realm of what you have pre-determined is possible?

Let's allow the Inner Teacher to form us anew. Let's open wider, and then still wider.

What would happen if you were so open that you received everything in your experience without any resistance? Everything. What if you paused, and let go of the need to touch everything with your instant right/wrong, good/bad judgment, and just let it sit there, not to be acted upon, or run from? Are you willing to try it, even for a minute?

You may find that what might be initially judged a difficult tare, was actually wheat, and what seemed like attractive wheat, was a tare... Let's receive what comes our way, judgment-free, and not act until Grace beckons you to gather and burn, or gather and reap. Grace doesn't need you to judge. It knows and reveals your path.

Relentless. In what areas in your life are you relentless? Are you relentless in your yielding to Thy will be done?

A friend the other day shared that she recently felt the unmistakable presence of Oneness like never before. It has literally transformed her view of relationships and experiences ever since. How did she do it? By "relinquishing any sense of control, and deep listening to Grace." Relentless surrendering...

When awakening through practicing unlearning, we begin to See, Listen, and Respond in fresh transformational ways. This Unlearning Insight will focus on Seeing. The next two will highlight Listening, and then Responding.

Seeing

Here you see what you are not conscious of through questioning that which keeps you locked in your current dream. This seeing alone does not make it go away. In fact, becoming conscious of lies within your habits can at first make them seem more real, because you may mistake them for being you.

An important part of the seeing is to become aware of the dream's impersonal nature. The ego is completely unoriginal, and displays common patterns with everyone. As you recognize the egoic blueprints, it becomes natural to let them go. This releasing creates a space for your hidden wholeness and divine oneness to emerge.

If instead of this process, you deny the presence of the egoic model, and go right to the absolute, there can be a danger of spiritual layering. This does not get at your core issues, and can create an illusion of a spiritualized ego. Here you may start to feel really good about yourself because you are so spiritual, but your new insights may not have taken root and transformed your listening and responding.

Listening

After we have begun unlearning through Seeing and recognizing egoic patterns in the way we illustrated above, we have created a space for deep Listening.

Our focus here is to not rely on what we have already figured out. That was fine for the past, but this moment is new. So, instead of rehearsing a litany of previously used truths, you listen beyond the mind. Here you begin by consciously acknowledging that you don't have an answer, as you open to the presence of Grace.

This stage makes the mind extremely uncomfortable because you are consciously entering the unknown. The Inner Teacher, or still small voice, is always there for us, but we may tend to tell it what we know, instead of opening ourselves in humility and really listening.

How each of us does this is an individualized matter. I will often ask God: What do I need to see right now? I then listen in the first person and take notes on what I hear. Sometimes it is a question and answer dialogue, and sometimes I am just listening and taking notes the entire time. I call it taking dictation. This activity always reinforces my unbreakable oneness with divinity. And, I receive what I am ready to hear from Grace.

Responding

The inspired Seeing and Listening that we illustrated above, is useless if we don't put what we hear into action. The words "listen" and "obedience" come from the same base word. So, are we willing to respond to what we hear with hit-the-street practical actions? Are we willing to commit to what we have heard?

There can be resistance showing up at each of these three stages, but this one is often the most aggressive because here we are acting our way into a new way of being. We are literally saying "No thank you" to the ego, and "Yes" to what we have seen and heard from Grace.

A vital aspect of this awakening process is to see it as not a one shot deal. We are opening to Seeing, Listening and Responding daily. We are given our daily bread this way. The tendency of the mind is get some great bread, and then try to store and preserve it in case you need it in the future.

Instead, we are consciously leaning into being the presence of Truth, moment-by-moment. It becomes completely natural to have all our actions driven by, and delivered through, Grace.

Tired of detours?

Grace guides us with unending exactitude. It always has and always will.

When your mind drifts away from the lucidity of the divinely natural order, and you are not sure what to do, or you are deeply yearning for direction, then what? Wholeheartedly open to, and listen for, the voice of Truth.

If the answer is not instantly clear, trust in, and act from, whatever comes next. It can show up in any form: a thought, a feeling, an action, something we see, or hear. It could come from within us, from another, in nature, etc.

But here's the key: KEEP LISTENING AND RESPOND-ING.

When seeking direction you don't go to your GPS and get one clear message and then stop paying attention. Grace is not a one shot deal. It guides you all the way home, and beyond…

Decision-Making

When you have an important decision to make, do you try
some (or all) of these exhausting scenarios?
- You work madly, trying to figure out what to do
- You feel nervous that you might make the wrong choice,
  which could have tremendously negative consequences
- You feel like you don't want to disappoint others who have
  expressed a preference
- You are afraid you will miss an amazing opportunity if
  you make the wrong choice
- You try to cover every conceivable base, to make sure you
  don't miss any opportunity
- You constantly seek out others with more experience, to
  ask what they think you should do
- You feel like the choice will set a life-direction that will be
  hard to change
- Your cost-benefit analysis reveals nothing conclusive, so
  now you are really stuck
- You ruminate over it continually, but make no progress on
  taking the decision
- You try prayer and usually hear nothing

Approach #2
Your role is not a decision-maker. Your role is to:
- Willingly embrace transformation
- Acknowledge that your conditioned mind does not know
  what is best for you (or anyone)
- Consciously turn all your decisions over to God
- Humbly listen for direction
- Obediently follow what you hear
- Trust your co-existence with Life
- Do this every day

If you have not practiced Approach #2 enough so that you feel confident turning your decisions over to Grace, use the next opportunity to learn how to do just that. It may just be more important than the outcome of the decision!

P.S. Next time you have a significant decision to make, first ask yourself: Which approach will I use?

If you yearn to be used by Grace in bigger service to mankind, then you need to let Grace drive all your actions right where you are now.

The Golden Spiral*

As the nautilus grows,
a partition appears
to seal off the previous chamber.
It can't go back
to that which it has outgrown,
but it can use the past
to pump gas into its spiral-chambers
to adjust its buoyancy.

Like us,
we are devoted
to living from the divine order
of Truth's fractal.

We can't go back
to that which Life has sealed off.
But, we can allow
the truth of our new perspective to permeate
the view of our past chambers,
and adjust our buoyancy.
That which used to weigh us down,
can be seen through
the weightless substance of Grace.

May this shell remind you that
Life is lived
in only one direction: Now.
We need not hold any
cherished opinions, fixed positions or guilty regrets.
We need not be "right."
We need only hold this one space:
Thy will be done.
It is that, to which we surrender.

Life is a classroom or a prison.
The only prison is the delusion
that you can exist
in chambers that are sealed off,
or yet to be formed.
You can't go there,
so don't even bother dreaming you can!

Live now!
Show up now!
Be now!

*The shell on the cover of this book is a chambered nautilus.

<u>Take One</u>: Noticing in Nature's Classroom

1. Nature is here to teach us.

2. There is only one infinite nature. It has an underlying order to it that, as much as we try, we just don't get. And that's wonderful! Who says we need to be able to understand everything?

3. Nothing in nature ever leaves nature. Where could it go? To our view, it just changes forms and goes right on without missing a beat.

4. Nature is always celebrating and being itself, because it does not have a deceptive consciousness to think it should be any other way.

<u>Take Two</u>: Today's Lessons from the Classroom

1. Life is here to teach us.

2. There is only one infinite Life. Life has an underlying order to it that, as much as we try, we just don't get. And that's wonderful! Who says we need to be able to understand everything?

3. Nothing in Life ever leaves Life. Where could it go? To our view, it just changes forms and goes right on without missing a beat.

4. Life is always celebrating and being itself because it does not have a deceptive consciousness to think it should be any other way.

Do you think that you know what is best for you? That may be true to some degree within your extremely limited frame of reference and finite options in your consideration set. In this worldview, there is the constant pressure to try and influence or control the outcome so you get what you think you want and deserve.

Option #2: Do you like Grace-driven surprises? How about opening to the Kingdom of Heaven on earth: allowing Life to unfurl you like a blossom in the sun?

The presence of Grace is unmistakably real. Time stops, location vanishes, and all that exists is a love that is so pure, simple, and clear that you find yourself fully quenched.

When listening to Grace, you don't go where you are needed, you go where you are called. You are needed everywhere. Saying yes to every need will bankrupt your life-flow.

To go where you are called you just have to listen to the one Voice as it directs you moment-by-moment. This divine Yes reveals a life that is detour-free and abundant. The outside stimulus may never change, but what you listen to and how you respond, reveals your experience.

If Grace drove all your actions, would you ever be concerned about an outcome?

If you are anxious about an outcome, perhaps you believe there is something other that Love in control.

Grace, the activity and voice of Love, shows up in the most transformative way you are ready and willing to experience it.

In this space there are infinite possibilities of blessings, and the best ones will be chosen and unfolded for you. Here you are giving Grace complete access to your deepest desires, by releasing all will. No pressure, just the effulgence of living in constant gratitude.

Chapter 3

Exploring
the Unknown

What happens when you think about any deep question, like: "What am I, beyond how I have always identified myself?" and you don't have an answer? Our minds are conditioned to hear "I don't know," and either think we should know, or figure we should leave the question.

How about hearing "I don't know" and beginning to celebrate?! "I don't know" means, "in my current way of thinking about things, I am left without an answer." Precisely. Instead of seeing this as the sad end of the road, how about viewing it as the beginning of a vast field of yet-to-be-discovered possibilities...?

Could it be that that space of awe is Life's answer to your question?

The only thing gained by thinking that you have the one right way to Truth (or anything really) is alienation of all those who have a different perspective. This stance repels others and isolates you in an impenetrable cocoon of self-righteousness.

An alternative is to think that you have a way to Truth that works for you today, and so does everyone else. This stance embraces others, honors everyone's journey, and leaves us all open to revelation.

The path of improvement and the path of transformation are not the same path. The first requires continual steps within the known. The second requires continual leaps into the unknown. School mostly encourages and rewards the first. Life demands and celebrates the second.

What would shift in your approach if you saw life less as a building process and more as an excavation and revealing?

You can think your way into a new way of acting. You can act your way into a new way of thinking. You can surrender yourself into a new way of being. These are not mutually exclusive.

The point is, to be open to something new through your thinking, acting and surrendering. Same old, same old, is not a viable option for awakening. What does new look and feel like for you?

A re you interested in awakening to the innate freedom that is your Being?

It makes sense to me that to awaken from something, and then to something, a first step is to be conscious and observant. What you are becoming more aware of is this concept called "self:" the thoughts, beliefs and feelings you most frequently identify as you.

When you watch it, you will likely see that it is caught in repetitive patterns or cycles of thought and action, which lead to frustration, confusion, sadness, and suffering. This thing you have been watching is what you are awakening from: that which you are not. So, this is not your identity, it is your 'miss-identity.' You have 'miss-identified' your identity.

That's actually great news: your identity is not leading you to suffering.

In the previous Insight we looked at our desire to awaken to our divinely unlimited nature. We emphasized the importance of self-awareness, and realizing that you are not the self that you observe caught in destructive patterns.

If you try to guide yourself to awaken by figuring out what you need to do next, you are pretty much guaranteed to take a detour. This is because you are using the mind that is caught in the cyclical conditioning, to awaken itself.

The need is to go beyond the mind you are awakening from. This may sound impossible, but it is deceptively simple.

What we often don't realize is that if you have this yearning to awaken, Grace is already guiding you. You did not create the yearning. It is coming from within you. So, you go to this yearning, the presence of Grace, and let it guide you.

If you feel this yearning a lot, then you will likely be inspired to do a lot. If you feel the yearning a little, then you be led to do less. Either is fine, just do what feeds this yearning, and don't try to force it. Let Grace ripen you.

To experience more of your selfless nature, notice how often your mind tries to control the way things turn out.

This will help you differentiate between the personal, self-contained, "It's all up to me!" self, and your divine Selfhood.

The personal self wants. The divine Self witnesses.

The personal self, trusts only what it can influence. The divine Self trusts what it cannot influence, because it knows that what God creates is governed completely: now and forever.

When these are seen and felt side-by-side in consciousness, the true blossoms and the imposter wilts.

The path of peace is discovering an ever-widening affectional consciousness in yourself, as Grace impels you to walk into your dark spaces, where your mind says you can't love…and your burgeoning heart says, "Oh yeah? Watch me!"

What if, instead of seeing yourself as a person, you saw (and felt) yourself as a field of Love?

Ask yourself: How would a field of Love respond in this situation? What would a field of Love do for a living? What would a field of Love bring to the activities of this day? Would a field of Love judge another (sounds weird to even hear it)?

Perhaps we are individual fields of Love, flowing together from One Infinite Green Pasture...

Once on a 3-day solo-vision quest in Utah, a fly landed on my knee as I sat in deep stillness in a dark red canyon. As I cherished and felt its beauty and oneness with Life, it let me gently stroke its back three times.

When it flew up and landed on my knee again, this time facing me, I very slowly moved my finger up to it. It stepped forward and took its leg and gently stroked my fingertip. Ever since then my purpose has been to see the Oneness of all life through an affectional consciousness.

What is sacred?

Could it be
that you are
so at one with the Divine
that you don't recognize its presence?

Could you be
looking for it so hard
that you miss it
because it is like your finger
looking for your hand?

Are you caught
thinking you have to do something
to get Love to show up?

What if the wait was over?

Ever notice how much time and energy your mind puts into wanting to specifically know how your needs will be met? We imagine what this could look like, and then get concerned when it does not unfold in the sequence we expect. This future-seek can be a full time job. The only pay check from this employment is anxiety, exhaustion and immobility.

Next time this comes up, just recognize it as a dead end. Instead, open your heart to God by asking, "What do I need to see right now?" Take notes on what you feel and are told.

You will find you are fully employed: listening and responding to Grace. There is nothing more natural and fulfilling.

W hat if:

- There is a primal order to Life that is so infinite that it is impossible to be outside it?
- This divine order is so infinite that it is impossible to influence or control it?
- This eternal order is so infinite that it is impossible to understand it?
- No matter what you do, you can't mess it up: you can't be out of order?
- The path of least suffering is to yield to that natural order?

If all that is true, what would you do?

W hen your believing, transitions to knowing, there are no longer any questions that "need" answers. Curiosity shifts to awe!

We have built a conceptual world that we feel secure within. We give meaning to everything in our world, and this meaning is based on our past. We are recycling our lives; bringing the past into the present, moment by moment. Most of this is unconscious.

The challenge comes when our world starts to crack, feel hollow, and unfulfilling. At the same time, if we allow ourselves to be really still, we may feel something within us calling us to go beyond our normal way of thinking and acting. How can we do that when we have spent 99.9% of our lives using past concepts to make sense of reality?

The door into the Unknown opens by honestly admitting (and embracing), "I don't know." Find the part of you that is not yet born, and listen there.

Is it possible that you try to control your life because you are afraid that if you don't, you will be without something you want?

Really? It would then follow that to get what you want you have to control people and situations.

Have you tried this approach? If so, how's it been working for you? If not, ask anyone who has tried it.

The reason you don't have to take control of situations, others, or even yourself, is because it is redundant. Grace has already taken it.

You get to watch and be, Grace-in-action.

Ever notice how when we feel a lack of peace, or even a lull in activity, we often go to food to try to feel better, or fill the gap? This can happen before we are even aware of it. We tend to eat our way through our days.

Of course, this never really satisfies us, so what do we do? Eat more. Then one day we find ourselves feeling addicted to disturbance-driven eating.

Another option? It sounds funny, but when a disturbance or lull arises, notice it in stillness (mental and physical), without letting anything pass by your lips. Then notice what comes up for you when your snacking routine breaks…

You are now entering new territory. Enjoy the scrumptious view!

Feeding Yourself

Do you put a lot of time and effort into thinking about and consuming food? Are you as devoted to feeding yourself spiritually every day as you are with physical food?

Consider these questions:

- Where is feeding yourself spiritually on your daily priority list?
- Have you recently thought about what a healthy and fulfilling spiritual diet would be like for you?
- Are you feeding your heart so you feel and experience your intimate oneness with all beings in Love?
- What best nourishes your heart?
- Do you feed yourself spiritually less, the same, or more often than you do physically?
- Do you consume the same spiritual food everyday? Is it nourishing you? Is it ever dry, rote, or abstract?
- Do you look forward to your spiritual meals?
- Are you feeding and strengthening your ability to respond to your deepest yearning, your purpose in life, your calling?
- Does your feeding support you living in your "zone?"

Cheers!

You are not something that can have something in you: something good or bad. You don't have life (or death) within you. You don't have health (or sickness) within you. You don't have love (or hatred) within you. You don't have peace (or stress) within you.

You are not a container that can hold anything. So what are you? The I am that the one I AM is being.

Whatever you are ready to receive into your experience, you will receive. Are you ready for the Divine order? Do you really want it?

Everything needs to be released. What if when a new insight came to you, your response was to appreciate it, use it, and release it? Instead, most of us grasp and save. We appreciate it, memorize it, categorize it, file it away in case we need it later, and then fill closets, basements, storage spaces, hard drives and... why?

Are you afraid you won't have something when you need it? What are you relying on for your clarity, inspiration, peace and security? Everything needs to be released.

Whatever you need, will be there when you need it. This is beyond memory. This is the very fabric of the Universe. All is One. Forever connected. How about trusting in, and releasing to divinity, to provide for all your needs?

A re you involved with spiritual education through parenting, grand parenting, mentoring, teaching Sunday School, church work, or other venues? What is your approach to this sacred work?

There can be a tendency in the mind to make religion and spirituality about following rules and do's and don'ts, so that we get on God's good side: kinda like setting up God in a Santa Claus image where He is checking His list to see who is naughty or nice.

How much of your educating involves helping others form and explore their unique and unknown relationship with the Divine through direct contact with Love? If you are not sure how to do this, awesome! What a wonderful question to be in, and to open up with others.

Every time you recognize the impersonal nature of how the ego works, you wake up from its spell, and Truth is more available in your experience. Unlearning the ego in this fashion requires moving closer to that which scares you. A mirage only keeps us captive from a distance. As you move closer to it, it vanishes.

Is there a developmental approach to experiencing spiritual awakening? I don't see awakening as a slow walk up a long hill in hopes of reaching the top.

I see it rather as a series of leaps to which you surrender. Each leap asks that you be open to a new view of yourself that is at one with Thy Will Be Done. In that space, the you that needs to be developed diminishes, and the you that already is, is revealed.

Simple Reliance

When you believe in many,
you don't completely trust
the Unknown,
so you try to control the known.

You try to figure out
how to create and manage
an ideal world for yourself,
working endlessly to sustain it.
You become attached
to people and things
and states of consciousness.
You are constantly scheming
and anxious about the future.

When you understand there is just One,
you completely trust
the Unknown,
so you release the known.   •

You have nothing to figure out
or sustain.
You have no concerns
or attachments.
You are not complacent
because you are being fully lived
by and as Love,
in service to all.

When it is time for something to fall away, the Presence that is leading us forth brings this awareness to consciousness. According to our plan, we may think the timing is wrong, and thus clutch and grasp tighter because we need it, want it, or don't know what we would do or be without it.

When we are unlearning, if there is pain, it does not come from dismantling the old model. It comes from the resistance to letting go. Releasing control always brings freedom, as we learn to trust our oneness with the Unknown.

When I am conscious that I don't have some things figured out, it leaves me anxious and somewhat open to being influenced by the Divine. I give the parts that I don't feel clear about to God, and I take care of the rest.

When I am conscious that I don't have anything figured out, it leaves me completely open to, and relying upon, the Divine. I give it all to God: what I am clear about, and fuzzy about. I take care to be conscious of surrendering, and watch God act through me and as me.

The first path leaves me tight, calculated, and stressful. The second path leaves me relaxed, and not able to stop smiling.

Exploring the Unknown

Chapter 4

Effortless
Takes Effort

Each of us is in a pas de deux with the Divine.

You are in perfect sync with the music of Soul. You are being led with the lightest of touch as you yield to the presence of infinite strength in each move. You and your Partner both know the choreography because it is that which resonates in your heart.

You are lifted when needed, and allowed to go solo when called for. But, while it looks like solo, the whole time you are still in an immaculate pas de deux. (Never forget that.)

You are living an unbreakable bond that unites and ignites those watching to want to dance our dance with our universal Partner.

You can never lose your balance because your Center is everywhere. As you yield to the on-going moment of grace, you realize there is only the dance.

There is only one infinite pas de deux.

Care to walk with me into Being?

Feel into One.
Open to Allness:
borderless Reality.
No plot plans or property rights.

Let yourself gentle-down into soft.
Breathe in
and exhale through all your pores.
Relax into the Unknown Love...
Allow your questions to rest without answers.
All of them.
Give your mind a holiday.

Grace is revealing us
with an affectionate intelligence
that governs all life simultaneously.
Can you enjoy it
without needing to know how it works?
You actually distinguish
only a microscopic speck of reality,
and even that
is a flickering, transient view in time.
And yet, understanding so little,
you are in this moment,
brilliant.

Notice how effortlessly you are being.
You don't try to be.
You can't not be.
Being is all there is.
One Being.
Feel (not think about) how you are being
an inexhaustible dimension
of the Dimensionless.

Unlock how calm you are
when you notice Being.
No anxious judgments,
just a sweet awareness
of the radiance of Now.
It's like feeling the sun warm you
from the inside out.

Release everything
to the one Being,
and experience Love being you
and all.

The seeker is a passing sense of self that only exists when
you are dreaming you are separate from something you
desire. As you awaken to realize that everything you have ever
yearned for you already include, as the consciousness of the
All and Only, the seeker disappears.

When there is nothing to seek, there is no seeker.

Unlearning Exercise

Can you think of someone who has done something to you such that you have decided that they are not lovable? What would they have to do in order for you to decide to love them?

At one level, you may believe that everyone's true nature is the expression of Love, but for some reason you may not be feeling and expressing love in this case. Unlearning involves spiritual inquiry: the willingness to really go into these questions and uncover (unlearn) the impersonal beliefs that are pinning these judgments to your experience. It involves questioning their veracity.

Once you are conscious of the core convictions that are keeping you from loving someone, you can ask yourself if they are true, and discern what clutching on to these beliefs is doing for your happiness, health, and peace. How's withholding love working for you?

You can then ask yourself: what would it take for you to feel and express genuine love to this person?

Someone practicing unlearning will take the time to actually write out responses to this exercise, not just think about it a bit. Uncovering your current drivers becomes more important than trying to maintain a facade that all is well... This kind of unlearning process will consciously and unconsciously allow your actions to be driven less by ego, and more by Grace.

Some Questions to Consider

- How much effort does it take to experience Grace? Is it effortless?

- Was Jesus' life effortless? How would you characterize his efforts?

- Consider the moments in your own life where you have been completely in the zone, where you have felt Life flowing through you and as you... How would you characterize your efforts? Did you make any efforts to prepare for these sacred moments?

- How would you describe your current efforts in relation to experiencing Grace? Are they working for you?

Simply Love

Any effort put into
wishing people were different,
can instead be put into
seeing and loving them
without any conditions or expectations.
When you are completely filled
with loving what is,
the wishing will be a distant memory,
if even that.

We love.
Not to get.
Not for an intended outcome.
Not to change anything.
Not because someone needs it.

We love because
Love is our nature.
We are love.
Trying to do or be anything else
will always leave us feeling
empty.
(Thank goodness!)

Think of a recent challenging experience (or incident) you went through. How much of that experience are you still carrying with you, stewing over it? The ego's role is to get us to dwell on how things should be different than they are. If you want to take a break from the ego, even for two seconds, feel what it feels like to need nothing to change.

In that space, there is no human will, no ego. It has no role. The focus is to let yourself into the realm where the suggestive will is abandoned. Feel that presence. This is very different than the exhaustive approach of trying to destroy the ego through battling it.

Clarity is not something you eventually arrive at. It is inherent and presently available in your being. It is not an accumulation of knowledge. It comes more from understanding how little you know, than how much you know.

Just who do you think you are? Really.

We hear this a lot: "I am stuck" (in this job, this lack of a job, this relationship, this lack of a relationship, etc.).

When you feel stuck, what actually is stuck? Is it you, your changeless, nameless identity, the full expression of infinite Intelligence, or is it the concept of you that your mind is holding onto?

It is these false, limited self-perceptions that we all identify with that we get to unlearn.

Here is one small shift, which can cause you to take a conscious pause, and aid your unlearning. How you use the words "I am" can help you be more aware of what you are identifying with. Here are a couple of examples of how I practice this:

- "I am noticing that Sandy feels stuck," vs. "I am stuck."
- "I am noticing that Sandy feels tired," vs. "I am tired."

The "I" in the first half of these statements is me: the consciousness of Truth. It notices the feelings present. This sounds a little strange because we are so used to thinking we are our feelings. Feelings come and go all the time, but you are always here.

Try it out, and notice the space opened by Grace, for the authentic you to emerge.

A problem with having goals is that there is a tendency to think you will be happier, or more fulfilled, or more peaceful, or more _____ (you fill it in) when you achieve your goal.

There is nothing inherently unhealthy about goals; it's just that when we attach a future heaven to them, it leads us astray.

Can you find a way to work on something that involves a goal, without leaving the fullness and abundance of each moment?

Can you discover the deep abiding joy in whatever you are doing? Life is too precious to miss a moment!

Do you ever feel like a slow learner? Would you like to learn more quickly and thoroughly the first time around?

One main reason we often don't learn quickly is because of the delay between the event and self-inquiry about the event. The closer the self-inquiry to the time of the occurrence, the quicker the lesson. Here's an example:

Let's say you went through a weekend with your family (or friends, or business colleagues, etc.). You can ask yourself: Were there any stressful moments in the weekend? Did I form any judgments about someone or myself as a result of the interactions?

If the answer is "Yes," then you could inquire into those judgments right away. See if you can discern if they are really true, or if they are stories you created.

When we are not aware of the judgments, we tend to imbed them in our storage house of unquestioned assumptions and carry them with us. They become part of our modus operandi and therefore negatively influence all future interactions.

This then turns into a mine we have ignorantly planted that could blow up next time we tread in a similar situation. It often results in us blaming others, increasing suffering, and delaying the learning even further.

Regularly taking time for honest self-inquiry can pay huge dividends in every area of our lives.

If you are using your mind to awaken through diligence and discipline, it can be helpful, but it won't take you all the way. You must engage your heart and be the love that will leave everything for Grace.

People often wonder how much effort to put into their spiritual practices.

My sense is that Grace will use whatever you show up with. If you are motivated to be diligent and disciplined, then Grace will flow through that channel. If you are motivated to be more spontaneous, then Grace will use that.

Is one better than the other? The question is a decoy. It is the mind asking the question so that it can try to master something and replicate it. It is not about perfecting a practice so that you can control the outcome.

Life is evolving as you. You can't make yourself evolve quicker than you are, any more than a tree can speed up its development. What your practices can do is remind you to be conscious, open to each moment, and willingly embrace transformation in the Unknown.

Let go of the wheel, and let Grace drive you.

The number one temptation, to which we need to be alert, is to think of reality as: God, and then, man. There are not two: God being one, and you being another. This can be very subtle because we don't have effective languaging to describe Oneness. Here's today's attempt to point to the Oneness of reality:

You are not a separate noun, lost among a sea of billions of other struggling nouns. You are the "ing" of the one infinite Verb. For example:

- God is the Sing, and you are the singing (not the singer).
- God is the Love, and you are the loving (not the lover).
- God is the Act, and you are the acting (not the actor).

When you are just one of the multitudinous nouns, you naturally adopt the consciousness that relies on yourself for everything. When you are the expression of the Verb, you are indissolubly at one with It. You are the way God shows up.

I played golf with our son today, and the best shots were the ones in which I did not try to make the ball go extra straight or super far. When I did try to do that, it was not pretty.

When I got 'egoing' out of the way (the desire to try to control things for an exact intended result), and let my authentic swing arrive, effortless energy appeared. It felt like I was completely at one with the club, ball and swing, alive in that moment, not trying to add anything or make something happen.

I was the swinging not the swinger: the activity of Life, not a separate being struggling to master a skill.

Ever notice how everything in your world seems to revolve around you?

What if it didn't?

Until She Remembered

The whispering mist
can entice you to *think*
you have a *mind* of your own,
with which you have to
figure everything out.

The whispering mist
can trick you to *think*
you have a *life* of your own,
with which you have to
provide for your own well-being.

The whispering mist
can seduce you to *think*
you have a *love* of your own,
with which you have to
decide whom to share your affection.

The whispering mist
can then suggest that
you braid these thoughts into a single strand,
and wrap yourself so tightly in them
that you *feel*
you have an *emptiness* of your own,
with which you have to wait for it to be filled by

some one...   some thing...   some place...

The whispering mist
would cause you to think and feel
you are separate,
even abandoned.

You are so used to companioning with this void
that you have christened it with a name: me.

Your sister, the great river, Clarity,
has also experienced
the challenge of whispering mist,
as she wandered seemingly endlessly…

Until she remembered
her source in the pure mountain spring,
and saw
that through all her traveling,
she ultimately joined the sea.

Until she remembered
that she was connected at both ends
to something BIGGER,
which began before…
and continues after…

Until she remembered
that what connects before and after
is the current, the now.

It is her *yielding*
to the current that runs through her, and as her,
that now gives her direction and purpose.

Clarity's commitment to her purpose
has revealed
her path…   her pace…   her peace…

Now, she sees herself carried
every moment
as an endless flow of fearless Life.

Picture yourself in awe of a breathtaking sunset. You are completely caught up in a total appreciation of the matchless beauty in front of you. In those moments you have no sense of a "self" that is watching this. The "me" disappears in the expression of awe. How does this feel? Exhilarating, peaceful, almost beyond words...

This is an example of a love that has lost a consciousness of self. This same "selfless" love can naturally flow toward anyone or anything in our experience that we allow it to. Loves creation is everywhere, and is that beautiful!

When you are thinking about what to say, or what to write, or what to do, Grace waits to take you into a room beyond the padded cell of anxious circular thinking, where you leave all the ruminating behind.

It is there that you allow yourself to reach into the unknown space in your consciousness that is forever happening right now for the first and only time. It is that Source that is flowing forth as your life, to which you are yielding. Why would we ever want to speak or write or act from anything other than this All-Wise fountain of Grace?

Just trust.

L ife is unfolding itself as your being this and every moment. You don't have any choice in the matter. You are the way It shows up.

What you get to do is yield to the perfectly intelligent flow of Grace, or willfully dream that you are running your life.

With Grace you are given the clarity:
- to know what you need to know to live authentically each moment
- to trust that whatever you need to know about the future you will be given the information in the exact moment you need it
- to not waste time wondering about anything else!

If I watched you objectively for the past year, to what would I see you were committed?

Is developing a conscious relationship with your authentic Self, your divine heritage, a priority to you? Is this the time to revisit the effectiveness of your spiritual practices? If so, here are some questions to consider:

- Do they help you experience an authentic, dynamic, awakened relationship with the one I AM?
- Do they encourage unlearning: exposing what you are not, and revealing what you are?
- Do they feed and nurture you to live from a purpose?
- Do they foster a deeper sense of surrender to and reliance upon the One?
- Do they cultivate a communicative relationship with Grace?
- Do they support your ability to sit alone in silence and be completely at peace?
- Do they help you awaken to what you already have and are in Truth?
- Do they assist you to live authentically?
- Do they open you to remove judgment from your mind and live from your heart with radical, unconditioned kindness?
- Do they help you go beyond what you know, and rely upon revelation?

Not all practices may do all these things, but this may be a healthy checklist to help you choose your practices for their effectiveness, not because you have always done them.

Do you ever have trouble finding the discipline to do that to which you have committed, e.g. an important project, or spiritual practices? If you try to muster more effort, more focus, more concentration, these may give you a short-term spike, but they are not sustainable. They are derived from the head-space. This kind of exertion can leave you feeling exhausted and drained.

When you are on your game, in your zone, and living from your purpose, being disciplined is not a chore. It is practically effortless. And any extra effort you put in is in service to what you love, so it does not feel forced or strained.

If you find the desired discipline waning, the need may be to reconnect with your heart-space. Remember what you most want in life, your deepest yearning, your authentic desires, your calling, what brings you the most fulfillment.

When those are clear and you let them impel you, any activity you are involved with can either feed this yearning, or be a radiant expression of it in service to mankind and Grace. This kind of effort often leaves you feeling refreshed, rejuvenated, and humbly grateful.

(If it was a physical activity like dance, you may feel like you left it all on the dance floor, but you are not depleted. You are peacefully pooped.)

If you love the view, you will wash the windows. Whatever unlearning it takes to keep the windows clean, I'm in!

We can never know what will happen in the next moment.

When we lose the need to know, an intuitive awareness arises that gives us exactly what we need.

When we release any sense of responsibility for having any (or all) of the right answers, we learn to trust a new kind of effortless knowing with everything.

It is this kind of opening to the Field of infinite possibilities, where we witness each moment blossoming with the option delivered by Grace.

How cool is that?!

You will never be understood precisely in the way your mind would like to be understood. It is not possible. No one else has your exact conditioning. It will never be a perfect match.

Any effort you put into being seen and liked by others in specific ways is like peddling a bike up a hill with its chain off: disappointing, completely exhausting, and fruitless. Instead of being upset with the other, see if you can just notice when this subtle insanity comes up for you.

Nature is so big (as in infinite) that nothing can stop it from expressing itself. Nature can't stop being.

What a perfect analogy for our coexistence with the Divine. Wherever God is, you are being expressed. Your divine nature is such that nothing can stop you from being fully expressed. Ever.

This is why, when you are in your zone, expressing your authentic Self, you transcend limitations. This is your natural (as in infinite) state of being revealing itself.

There's nothing wrong with wanting to help people (or the world). That's a natural feeling. It's just that as long as you see people as needing help, then you won't be helping at a transformational level.

You may help them improve, develop, or progress, which is fine, but there will be a sense of the personal you helping people in need.

Transformation is not something we do. It comes from completely yielding and surrendering to the Divine: going to Grace, see each as whole and one with Life, dwelling there, and watching the divine will and presence do what it does, with or without you.

If you are actively involved, it will be very clear that all the activity is the flowing of Grace. And, you will have no attachment to what any outcome should look like.

Simply Surrender

give up control
stop resisting
relinquish the need to be right
admit you don't know
agree to not judge
yield to joy
consent to this moment
accept everyone
allow gratitude to flow
embrace the darkness
defer to reality
feel freedom
breathe in and out
celebrate what is
grasp nothing
stop pushing
release everything
stand defenseless
fear nothing
walk in your truth
let grace land
resign to love
give in to peace

simply be

It is simple to be aligned with the Divine, because this is what we are.

To experience it, surrender to Grace by:
- Acting when it flows
- Listening when you hesitate
- Questioning when stress arrives
- Relying on the Unknown
- Remaining judgment-free during all of the above
- Abandoning this list if it ever feels like a prescription

Effortless Takes Effort

Chapter 5

The Gift of Non-Judgment

Are there any important areas in your life where you have decided that you know "the" right way to do something? If so, this may permeate your perceptions of others and subtly lead to thinking that you are better than those who don't understand or agree with your way.

This mindset unconsciously infiltrates all your interactions with others (including children). They can feel it, even if they don't know what it is. Something is just off. This is a cornerstone of isolation and war.

What if you made the shift to deciding you know "one" right way that works for you in this moment? This authentic mindset keeps you open to listening and learning continuously from everyone (including children). It leaves room for Grace. This is a cornerstone of community and peace.

Borderless Loving

Your heart cannot love
beyond the borders
of your consciousness.
Your borders are staked
by the conscious
and unconscious
judgments you hold.

Stories are an invasive species planted by errant seeds of judgment, and nurtured by a lack of Grace-driven self-awareness.

They infiltrate your consciousness and dramatize your relationships, success, health, and peace to the degree you believe them. The year-round fruit they bear is suffering.

Whatever you become aware of that is happening outside of you, is also going on inside of you. See if you can find it.

This may soften some judgments.

Life is like an eternal video, not a photograph.

When you create a judgment about someone from an experience, you have freeze-framed a view of reality, created a story based on your limited information, and then projected it as the new reality.

This activity moves you into a dream state where you think you are in control, and know what is going on. Link a series of these judgments together and your consciousness is completely removed from the divine reality. Result: your own current and/or future suffering.

Alternative: Watch Life unfold without needing to form judgments, opinions, stories, or beliefs. Let everything be as it is, and rest assured that you and everyone are governed by a Presence that does not need you to reinterpret and correct it.

Without a story, there is no storyteller. Your self-concept is wrapped around all the judgmental stories you tell yourself about your life. Here are just a few examples:

- My Dad should have treated me with _____.
- My Mom should have treated me with _____.
- _____ should not have happened to me.
- I should have known better than to _____.
- So and so doesn't like me because _____.
- I don't have value because _____.
- I wish my body was _____.
- I should be making more _____.

As you bring the understanding to these stories that they are simply fabricated beliefs, and not definitively true, an amazing thing starts to happen: the stories soften and melt, and with them your view of yourself as a confused, limited, mortal starts to dissolve.

Once you see that the stories are empty, the container holding the stories is no longer needed. What starts to shine forth is the authentic you that is free to see and experience life without anxious tension and hesitancy. Your smile naturally widens.

Our Rights

People have the right
to think whatever they want to
about you.

You have the right
to experience the freedom
of knowing that they are not
their thoughts about you.

Nothing is ever personal. If you think it is, even that is not personal. You are drawing from the conditioning of your mind. Your mind has been conditioned by multitudinous factors, and not one of them comes from you.

You are innocent, because you are not your mind.

When you notice, and let your awareness touch on whatever comes into your experience, it is not the same as accepting it as real and true. You are not making a belief out of it that needs to be rejected, denied, or accepted. If you see something that you think needs to be changed, you may have unconsciously already accepted that Reality is broken.

Instead, you create no story about it. It's like: a friend called. Not a good friend, or a bad friend. Not he should have asked more questions, or spoken less. Just notice: "A friend called."

You are dwelling in a consciousness that is not trying to make disharmony into harmony, the way you think it should be.

There is a ground or stage of Freedom upon which the mortal dance breathes in and out, comes and goes. Perhaps noticing allows us to experience how freedom is the reality, and the movie of mortality is just a flashing projection on the retina of the mind.

We are free.

Let's allow the healing vibrancy of Grace to reclaim every single decision we have ever participated in, leaving no room for regrets or blame... just pure, uncluttered, compassionate, redemption and celebration.

We don't condemn a toddler who falls while learning to walk. And, we don't now feel bad that we stumbled while emerging from crawling to walking. So, if you are looking at your past (even if the past was an hour ago), drop the "I should have known better" and realize you are still learning to walk.

Life is too precious to be spent in self-condemnation. Try gratitude for increased awareness instead.

Awareness vs. Judgment

Awareness rests gently on an object without impacting your view. It brings the object into consciousness while maintaining perfect equanimity. Try it out. Pick an aspect of yourself, like your body, and just notice it (this is not easy to do). Feel how light and free awareness is.

Judgment evaluates an object by leaving it changed in your view. It can bring it into consciousness causing you to feel disturbed or justified. Try judgment out. Judge your body (perhaps how it should be different in some way). Feel how heavy and burdensome judgment is.

Self-judgment leads to self-condemnation, which leads to self-destruction: a downward, depressing vortex of suffering.

By practicing self-awareness, openness is augmented, unlearning is expedited, and clarity becomes intuitive. You become an ego-free zone that allows your actions to be driven by Grace.

May you…

May you let
your thought sweetly rest
on whoever comes to consciousness,
without the slightest judgment,
or need for them to be different
in any way.

May you find
the quiet humility
to love them as they are right now,
and just for this moment,
may you feel
that this is enough.

May you include
in this Christlike embrace,
the one for you right now
that may be hardest to love.
This may be
the most precious gift
you have ever given
(and he or she has ever received).

May you know
that other's yearning hearts
are sending you this same gift,
even if their words and actions
don't match up.

May you accept
that all hearts are forever united
as One.

Whatever you judge as should not be happening, will get repeated in your experience in some form. Your judgment is the glue that holds it in your consciousness. It is actually your judgment that keeps you annoyed. But, the ego will convince you it is the situation.

Whatever you forgive and release may or may not get repeated in your experience. The difference is that when you have forgiven, what shows up has no sting for you. It is irrelevant.

The thought comes, "I am worthless. No one really cares about me." The thought is 100% harmless until you identify with it and believe it. Next time that kind of thought comes, notice that it arrived, be grateful you are aware of it, and set it down on the chair beside you.

For example, "Here's that thought again. You can sit over in that chair, while I continue on with my day without you." No battle. No judgment. Just the natural clarity to know what is true and what is not.

For the last year I have made a conscious space for a minimum of 20 minutes/day to sit in stillness and just notice my thinking.

No analyzing, synthesizing, evaluating, judging or believing any thought or feeling during that time. Just letting my awareness observe whatever comes to consciousness. No effort to keep anything there, or push something away. Just noticing.

One of the things I've realized is how my mind seems to be programmed against this. It's like its default space is either:
• Believing thoughts, interpreting them, creating judgmental stories, and trying to control the whole process, or
• Turning to memories, and hanging out there to condemn myself or scheme a better future.

Here are three insights from this practice (so far):

1. The conditioned mind habitually creates its own heaven or hell, independent of what is actually happening.
2. We become slaves to either chasing a slippery heaven, or trying to break out of cyclical suffering.
3. Through non-judgmental noticing, a space for Grace is created throughout the day that allows for a kind of knowing that intuitively relies on revelation.

Once upon a time there was a self-sustaining dream. It was not a good dream or a bad dream. It was just an innocent dream. All it knew how to do was dream, so it dreamt that:

- It would create something that it called a person or being.
- There would be a multiplicity of these beings.
- Each being would believe that it had a life of its own.
- Each being would randomly appear in the dream, and then disappear.
- Each being would try to do anything it could to make the dream better for itself.
- Each being would feel like it was deficient, and had to worry if its needs would be met.
- Each being would long to be needed and valued by each other being.
- Each being would seek peace in the dream.
- Each being was given a mind and senses to distract it, and to confine it to recognize only what was within the dream.

Because it was self-sustaining, the one thing the dream did not know how to do, was to awaken each being from the dream.

But, what the dream did not realize was that, independent of the dream, there existed one infinite, forever-awake Consciousness, which did not dream. And, that every limitation the dream ever created was already countered by this one Consciousness. And, this one Consciousness had the ability to awaken each dreaming being, by giving it unlimited access to Itself.

The dreaming beings would call this compassionate access, grace. When each dreaming being experienced grace, it would be introduced to its one infinite, authentic Selfhood, beyond the dream. Grace would show each being what was needed to unlearn the mind in the dream, and to awaken to the unknown Consciousness.

Grace's primary teaching was always the same: to help each dreaming being dedicate its heart to not judging anyone, or anything, in the dream. Through this simple unselfing process, all attachments were gradually dropped, and it would naturally awaken, as the I AM of Love.

•

Love's Gift

So I walk into Sunday School
and you have your head down on the table.
Strange…
I usually get an enthusiastic greeting and hug or high five.

Your friend says you are not feeling well…
I think, not the "you" I know…
You look up at me barely lifting your head
and yet smiling through your pain…
I feel cherished and seen.

We start class and you excuse yourself…
to the rest room to remove what won't stay down.

You come back. We are working away.
I hand you your sheet.
We are remembering our purpose in life.
You thank me, begin writing and smile again
through your yearning for health.
I am hugged again.

Soon, back to the rest room for more release.
You stay there for the rest of class.
As I leave the class and turn the corner,
you are sitting on a distant bench, hunched over.
Our eyes did not meet.

There is a sign on the bathroom door.
"Do Not Enter: Needs to be Cleaned"
I think, this is my daughter, this is our home…
mopping the floor and walls with bundles of TP…
this is not gross.
What would you not do to thank one
who has loved you so purely?

Small price to pay…
It all gets flushed.
A helper arrives to finish with a mop.
We are good to go.

I walk over to you and our eyes meet.
You beam a smile that says
"This stuff can't keep me from loving you."

I am blown away by your gift.
Indeed, you are Love's Gift.
That is my new name for you. Love's Gift.

Five days later on the flight home,
I am struggling with my perception
of how unreasonable a colleague is.
He is standing in the way of my precious outcome.
I am hunched over in pain, hating him for his views…

And then I remember what you gave me…
freely, even through your pain…
And I realize that this is all I want in life;
to give Love's gift.

So, I stop strangling my foe,
and start loving my friend.
I go beyond my sick feelings and
I give him Love's gift.
I realize that this is all that matters.
Take my money and whatever else you want.
It does not matter.
I am giving you Love's gift.
I am yielding to Love, and doing nothing more.
Peace floods in
as your gift has effortlessly mopped up and flushed
my indigestion.

And perhaps you thought that you missed
our Sunday School class.
Oh no. You were there.
You showed up beyond your struggle
and loved me.

You gave me yourself: Love's Gift.

Blaming another for your suffering is futile and insane. All it accomplishes is you feeling victimized and stuck.

It is vital that you own what is showing up in your life. "Own" does not mean you created the events in your experience. It means you are willing to inquire into how you are contributing to any suffering that is occurring this moment.

You don't focus on trying to control who or what walks across the stage of your consciousness. That's like trying to control the news in your town.

You let your awareness rest in what is occurring on your stage, knowing that whatever you see, (and whatever your mind wants to make it mean), there is a Divine Order that is infinitely bigger than you could ever understand, that is governing all in perfect harmony.

And when you find that your gentle awareness notices within you a stressful place where your mind thinks you or the news should be different, you inquire into the truth of that belief.

You don't judge the news or yourself for responding to the news. You love that you get to watch Grace untangle and re-order your mind's innocent thoughts, and restore your peace.

A Trail of Peace

When a judgment arises
and feels like it is your thinking,
give it pause,
with your full attention,
and feel if it leaves
a trail of peace in your heart.

If not,
just realize
that it came to pass,
and let it keep on passing.
No attachment,
no harm.

The transcendent simplicity of awareness, is that is does not judge.

This gives a whole new meaning to the vital importance of self-awareness in our effort to awaken to our innate oneness with all being in Love.

Advancing Degrees of Judgment

<u>Junior High</u>: Judging yourself and others
<u>Senior High</u>: Colluding with others about your judgments
<u>College</u>: Judging others for having judgments
<u>Masters</u>: Being conscious of your judgments and still retaining them
<u>Doctorate</u>: Correcting others about their judgments while keeping yours

What degrees have you earned? Is it time to unlearn?

Most (if not all) of us want to love unconditionally. It is not likely that is going to happen if we are not aware of how conditioned our mind is to be selective in our loving. If we use our minds to figure out who, how, and what to love, we end up evaluating and judging others and ourselves. This is completely wasted energy.

Alternative: Begin to explore what it means to have no conditions on your love. Zero. Feel what it might be like to love everything that enters your experience… the perceived darkness and the light!

Legalism in spirituality is defined as behavioral adherence to the letter of the law. If you maintain specific behaviors, you are in, and God will love and help you. If you don't, you are out, and God will not help or love you.

Ever notice how the "in" behaviors change over time as our cultures change?

Our institutions that practice legalism tend to turn people away from the very thing they are hoping to inspire people to love.

Where is the room for an authentic, non-judgmental conversation about topics in our yearning hearts? Where is the space that supports and encourages each individual to develop an active transformative connection with Grace? Isn't this what we really want?

Best in Show?

Do you have room in your heart
to let others have
their interpretation of Reality
that is just as real and right
as yours is to you?

And,
can you celebrate
that one is not more right
than another?

Is a rose more right than a lily?

To compare
would be to forget
that each is the way
Nature communicates.

The conditioned mind loves to try to be in control. It tries to put everything in its place so that it is not disturbed. In doing this it continually forms beliefs about the way things should or should not be.

Ever notice the difference between forming a belief about something vs. noticing it? With the forming of beliefs there is a continual effort to grasp, push away, deny, judge, and personalize our experience. Many of us are carrying decades of these kinds of accumulated beliefs.

When you notice something you are simply becoming aware of it. There is a gentle, light, non-judgmental resting, with no attempt to change or manipulate what you aware of. Awareness has no will.

Let's try it right now. Take a current event: someone got re-elected. Watch the mind instantly go to why this is great, or why it is the pits, and all the ramifications… !

Now, let that go. Just let your awareness rest on the fact: someone got re-elected…

Can you feel the difference? The emergence of a new space? A different kind of freedom? A field of possibility? It's like walking without baggage.

A sacred space emerges for Grace to appear, when you let awareness be enough.

The doorway into experiencing all you are, is through embracing all you are not. (At this point some of you may quit reading.) That's fine. ;)

Our tendency is to run from what we are not, but this usually means that it just momentarily leaves our conscious experience. Actually, we are still dragging it around behind us, and it will likely come rebounding back later and surprise us, because, " I thought I already handled that!"

When you embrace what you are not, you don't indulge it, you just sit with it, and see what happens if you don't try to fight it, or figure it out. By giving it this non-judgmental attention, you no longer grasp it, and in its own time it falls away. What emerges is the authentic experience that you are infinitely bigger than any lie could ever suggest.

This Grace-driven process never leaves you where it found you.

Finding Friendship

Think of a friend
that is hard to love right now.
Do you have the person in mind?
Now, pick one reason
that makes it difficult to love him or her.
Got one thing that bugs you?

How long has this thing
stopped you from loving them?
How long will it continue
to stop you from loving them?
Are you good with that?
(Apparently.)

Are you waiting
for them to change?
What if they never change?
Does that mean you will never love them?
(So far, that is accurate.)

How long will it be
until you decide
to love the person anyway?

Your withholding of love
is the source of your suffering.
It has absolutely nothing to do
with their actions.

Can you find
the place in your heart
that gets that?

It is a field of
innocent Stillness,
pure sanity,
that never learned how to judge.
It is there.
Your friend is waiting for you there.

Today I thought about a corporate executive I was judging for destroying the environment and the lives of innocent people. I asked God: "What do I need to see right now?" Here's how the dialogue went:

God: "Be the man you hate. Be him. (Long pause) Can you really hate him? Can you honestly feel anything but love for him? What happens inside you when you hate?"

Sandy: "I take a stand against Love. I proclaim to the world that I stand for the opposite of Love."

God: "How does that feel?"

Sandy: "Ludicrous. Insane. Repulsive. Inauthentic. I am so sorry. This is my brother. I am my brother. Evil is not in him. It is in my ignorant perception of him. This is not a viable option. I embrace the darkness because it cannot stop the love we are: the love I am, the love he is."

God: "Any evil that you personify, you get to unlearn. Be open to finding it in you so nothing unlike Love exists in you. Then, it will not exist anywhere else."

Need more time in your day? Become conscious to take any time you put toward judgment and the ensuing stories you then worry about and ruminate over, and simply stop. Put your foot consciously on the brake.

As your mind slows down and you put it in park, get out, close the door, and take a deep breath. Open your eyes. In front of you will be a newfound field of Grace? Take it in... It is a gift. You can get back into your activity whenever you want to, but this pit stop may change your life (or at least your day).

Chapter 6

Unlearning the Conditioned Mind

Spiritual awakening using an unlearning process involves subtraction rather than addition. With addition you continually try to add more spiritual understanding so that it floods your thinking and inspires you with new insights. It can feel very conceptual and intellectual.

With subtraction you become aware of what you unconsciously believe and do that leads you away from oneness, and into separation. Illusions are uncovered and egoic patterns are exposed. This can wrench your heart because you begin to see you may have been in a trance for decades.

The awareness of trance-living simultaneously reveals a heart-driven desire to awaken into something real and authentic. This fuels the courage to face transformation by opening to yet-to-be explored aspects of Reality. While this can be scary, you begin to feel yourself drawn into the chrysalis where Grace forms you anew. In the subtraction process there is no turning back, because what falls away is everything you thought your were. What is left is all you are and ever have been.

O nce upon a time you forgot you were dreaming, and thought you were a child. You started believing you were a separate being with a body of your own: "There I am in the mirror." Then you learned that your body has a name, an identity: "That is me."

Next you began to identify with things outside you, thinking they were yours and part of your identity: "This is my toy, my clothes, my family, my friends, my school, my team, my job, my money, my car, my lover, my religion, my country…" And looking internally: "These are my thoughts, my feelings, my beliefs, my opinions…" "It's all me and mine."

Along the way you learned that you needed to gather, protect, and defend all these things so you can preserve your self and your world. And, for a while, this felt normal, and may have worked for you…until it didn't. And, as it started to crumble, you found yourself struggling, confused, discouraged, in pain, suffering.

Your initial response was to work harder, try to do more, control more. But that didn't work. You then may have tried to use spirituality to "fix-the-broken me." But that didn't work.

If you can relate to this scenario, what are you finding that is helping you tangibly and consistently wake up from this dream?

Premise: (Continued from the previous Insight)
The whole story of this supposititious incarnation is a dream.

Transformative spirituality is intended to awaken you from the dream of duality, or separation from God and all life, to Oneness. It teaches you that all this is learned, and that, it can be unlearned. It is simply the way your mind has been conditioned. It's not good or bad; it's just the way it humanly works. It's not personal. Ever. So, there is nothing to judge or condemn.

You realize that all you are watching is a projection of the mind. You have stadium seating and surround sound in this theatre of separation. And, you see that your mind has been conditioned to think you are the lead in the movie, trying to control the plot to satisfy and save yourself, and even other supporting actors. Crazy stuff.

A huge (and often underestimated) step in awakening is when you begin to notice yourself in the movie. It all of a sudden dawns, "Wait. If I can notice my "self" in the movie, who or what is it that is doing the noticing?" This is the beginning of detaching your sense of self from the dramatic projection, and all its entanglements.

As you open to Grace, you wake up to the clarity that you aren't in the movie, or even creating the projection. None of it is you or yours. You are pure divine consciousness. The movie is an insane flashing mirage: an impossible, dysfunctional lie, that somehow you are a separate, finite, limited being.

The intention of every Unlearning Insight, in whatever form it takes, is to help you leave the theatre of belief in disconnection, and awaken as the presence of One Eternal Connection.

Insanity is believing in something that is not there (e.g. a false judgment), seeing something that is not there (e.g. your story about another), or denying the reality that is always there (e.g. Truth).

The unlearning process involves accepting that your mind has been insane, noticing where it is still insane, and celebrating that you are waking up from an insane dream!

Interesting how the mind resists what the heart lives on...

The mind wants to figure everything out so that it thinks it is in control of life. It wants to narrow down the possibilities and corral everything in.

The heart on fire doesn't need to know how anything will work out. It is overflowing with love as it watches Life reveal itself; new every moment!

We need to unlearn the mind, and free the heart to dance with Grace!

Paradox

In many ways
it's all about you.
Everything revolves
around your projection and perception.
It's imperative to own what is yours.

In many ways
it has nothing to do with you at all.
Thoughts come and go
without your beckoning.
Nothing is personal.
It's vital to practice non-attachment.

Both are true.
And the mind can find this confusing…

And yet,
when you are willing to listen,
Grace gently guides you
to just what you need to unlearn,
when you need it,
so you can awaken
to what you already are.

Ever notice how often your mind keeps returning to the same thought patterns like: judgment, condemnation, resentment, anxiety, indecision, self-doubt, etc.? It's like no matter what, these keep coming back.

In this way, the mind develops a conditioning for sameness. It may not like what it has, but it gets used to the consistency of it, and thinks that life is supposed be filled with human certainty.

Taking this mental model, the mind tries to create an ideal future state in which the undesirable is permanently removed, and the desirable is sustained. And, it feels great responsibility, and puts an enormous effort, into trying to achieve this. It will even attempt to use religion or spirituality to sustain this ideal state.

The mind is further conditioned to not question this approach, but rather, accept it as normal and natural.

Does this sound familiar? So how has it been working for you?

The problem with this methodology is that it will never work. Why? You can't control or sustain what happens in a dream. Everything comes and goes. It is a self-enclosed system: you are using the human mind to fix and create a perfect human mind. It is focused away from now, on creating a future heaven.

The next Insight opens up some alternatives to this deceptive habituation.

Following the previous Insight…here are some radical alternatives to trying in vain to sustain human states or conditions:

- Consciously notice and embrace the unfolding moment as it is happening
- Celebrate whatever is happening now by giving thanks and trusting there is good in it (even if it is not obvious)
- Love the freedom in that you don't have to have everything (or anything) figured out
- Whenever a question arises, take it first to Grace, and listen
- Become aware that your mind is dreaming by creating stories
- Notice the mind making judgments, and question them
- Instead of trying to improve a nightmare, recognize that you are not actually in it: you are not the sufferer in your experience
- Open to the part of you that is at peace no matter what is going on
- Realize that you are not your thoughts and feelings, and just consciously observe them
- Ask yourself: Who or what is it that can observe my mind?
- Allow Grace to choreograph and dance you

The mind will try to rifle through this list, check it off as done, and not really open to any of them. See if you can sit in stillness, and gently rest in whichever ones call to you. Listen to them, and let them move within you.

Each and all of these simple practices can walk you beyond the conditioned mind, and give you an original experience with unconditioned Consciousness.

When you are in egoic consciousness, you may think it is not a big deal, and that your actions are not really impacting much. This is because the effects of your actions are not always seen immediately. There is often a delay before you see the real damage.

Please remember: when you are letting the ego run the show, you have no ability to act in your own or another's best interest. At best, you are simply reinforcing the delusion of separation. At worst, you are planting tares in virgin soil that is hungering for wheat.

When you are averse to the ego and battling it, you are caught in it. When your vision is clear and you understand that the ego is just stories and abstractions about what is, then you are free. You let it tell it's stories but without giving it an audience, because you are not interested in the same old drama.

Change of Heart

I can't tell you
that the way you are acting
is making me upset or happy.
That can never be true.

I can tell you
that because of the way
I am miss-seeing you,
I am making myself upset or happy.

Strange that I would do that.

Why not
just feel you
as whole
and one with Love,
and be happy
no matter how you show up?

I'm on it!

When you are asleep and dreaming, the conditioning in your mind is making non-stop decisions. One moment you are skiing with a friend, then eating Chinese food, then reading a book, and on and on.

When you are awake and not aware of your thinking, this same conditioned mind may be making decisions for you. You may unconsciously find yourself saying or doing things that are not in your, or others, best interest. This is what Paul was experiencing when he wrote, "The good that I would, I do not: but the evil which I would not, that I do." (Romans 7:19)

To unlearn your conditioning, it helps to notice how the cycles and patterns of the ego operate. As this gets depersonalized, you lose self-judgment, and find your natural, innate, clarity emerging.

Life is unfolding us in a divinely natural order. When our minds second guess Life, we are shackled with 100% drama. Time to lose your mind.

Choosing Your Lens

Ever notice that when you choose a lens through which to see yourself, your entire perception conforms to that view?

Lens = Incompleteness
1. If you believe you don't have worth, you interpret the way people treat you as never enough to fill you up.
2. If you believe you are incapable, you continually judge your performance as not quite good enough.
3. If you believe you don't make a difference, you think that if you weren't here, no one would care.

Lens = Wholeness
1. If you believe you have worth, you get that the way people treat you tells you about them, not about you.
2. If you believe you are capable, you trust that you are doing your best, and that you can always learn and improve.
3. If you believe you make a difference, you are inspired to give and receive to your fullest potential.

Lens = The oneness of all Life
1. If you know that all life has worth, you love all life without conditions, regardless of how they are showing up today.
2. If you know that all life is capable, you don't judge or compare others since everyone is playing their part in one infinite Being.
3. If you know that all life makes a difference, you let Grace make all decisions and drive all actions.

When standing before a breath-taking sunset with a friend, you will look through one of lenses from the previous Insight. This will cause one of the following scenarios to be played out. You may find yourself:

1. Thinking not about the sunset, but about the friend and how you can present yourself to them in a way that they think you are really cool and together. Intended result: an ideal future together. Unintended result: you miss the moment.

2. Thinking somewhat about the sunset, but simultaneously hoping that the person appreciates you for being so nice to experience this wonderful moment with them. Intended result: beholding the sunset and increased gratitude for you. Unintended result: a lingering feeling that you didn't leave it all for the moment.

3. Being so in awe as you stand in front of the sunset with your friend, that this moment is all that is happening. You, your friend, and the sunset merge in Grace, as there is no self-consciousness interfering with the matchless unfolding of Soul. There is no intended result. Unintended result: Oneness experienced.

In the previous Insight we looked at three possible scenarios when we are in relationship with someone. We related it to watching a sunset together, but it can show up in any and every aspect of the relationship. The first is self-centered, or selfish. The second is unselfish. The third is selfless, or unselfed.

If you see yourself acting out the first or second scenario, the key is not to try to get to #3 as quickly as you can. The secret is to fully experience where you are, and ride through it consciously unlearning, with awareness.

To help you fully move through a stage vs. getting stuck there, you may want to ask yourself:
- How authentic do you feel in various relational moments?
- How does each experience leave you feeling? Is there an aftertaste of peace, anxiety, regret?
- Can you notice how your motives and actions resonate with the deepest peace that you can access?
- Can you find even a momentary stillness that exists within you that is not dependent upon anything someone else does? If so, rest in that presence occasionally.
- What do you really want in life?

The point of entrance to awakening is a conscious awareness of where you are right now. As you open to letting Grace live you, you will be permeated by a higher order that does not need your volition or help. Within this order, like a tree, some leaves you used to cling to will fall gently away. (And you won't even miss them.)

In continuing the theme from the last three Insights, someone asked: "What to do if the other person is selfish, but you are willing to do anything to make it work?" I thought we all could relate to the question.

What you choose to do depends upon many factors. I am clearly not going to tell you what to do, but we can open up how to discern what is authentic for you.

See if you can first notice which mindset you are acting from in this kind of setting: selfish, unselfish, or selfless. Be brutally honest with yourself. That in itself can be very revealing.

Next, when you are in the mindset of being "willing to do anything to make it work," ask yourself the first three questions from yesterday's insight.

- How authentic do you feel in these moments?
- How does acting this way leave <u>you</u> feeling? Is there an aftertaste of peace, anxiety, regret, etc.?
- Do your motives and actions resonate with the deepest peace that you can access?

What I'm encouraging you to get in touch with is your deepest sense of what is authentic for you, versus doing what you think another wants you to do. If you don't stay true to yourself, everything starts to atrophy.

The Heart's Freedom

When you allow yourself
to transcend personalizing thoughts,
you are not upset by anything.

All thoughts are homeless.
Each arrives spontaneously.
They don't come with a "me" nature.
There is no such thing as "my" thought or "their" thought.
You add the personal attachment.
Or not.

Thoughts do not arise from people.
You are not a creator.
You may entertain them,
fight them,
believe them,
release them,
or act in accord with them.
But, you don't own them.
They are not for sale.
They are not yours or anyone's.

You are that which exists before, during and after
any thoughts appear or disappear.

As this sense of "you" evolves,
you feel your heart's rebirth
as you become
the freedom and awe
of every moment.

If the conditioned mind is your normal operating system, then when Grace's invitation to live in YES arrives at the email box of consciousness, it is instantly seen as invalid, and get's filed into junk mail.

The unlearning process involves going through your junk mail, to see how much truth you may have consciously or unconsciously misfiled into oblivion. Could be time for a new operating system: your heart.

To what do you default when you need an answer to an important issue, your head or your heart?

Our conditioning in school and business, and what we see most modeled in the West, is a reliance on the head: the intellect. The head space tends to be analytical and places emphasis on figuring everything out. It creates endless stories and strategizes to control outcomes. It gives birth to anxiety because it tries to predict the future.

The heart space relies on listening to what brings you the greatest peace, to what calls you forth to express yourself fully, to what flows from your deepest yearning in life. It asks you to become very still, surrender your will, really listen, and let Grace reveal a direction or answer.

Needless to say, these two approaches will lead to very different paths. The head space tends to work exclusively in the human or horizontal realm with limited options. The heart space consults the divine or vertical realm, remembers there is one creation, and taps into infinite possibilities.

Just Unlearn It!

Most likely you don't need more of something to be happy, you need less of something.

- You may think you need more love, but actually you need to unlearn the belief that you are unlovable.
- You may think you need more money, but actually you need to unlearn the belief that you are deficient.
- You may think you need more self worth, but actually you need to unlearn the belief that you not worthy.

When awakening through unlearning, less is way more!

The more you lose interest in your self and all your stories and drama, the more you are ready for a transformed view of reality.

To break out of the same old patterns, you need to stop the same old response, no matter what it is. It has not worked. You need to move into a new space, like an explorer. What can you do to have a Grace-driven response vs. a humanly conditioned (even spiritual) reaction? Really listen into this space.

An important aspect of the unlearning process is to allow that which is unconsciously bothering you to rise to the surface, and become conscious. One way to unearth the uncomfortable feeling is to consciously sit with it without doing anything, and see what happens. This will typically not leave you where it found you.

Anything could occur next, but the key is, you will be entering new ground. This is the point. We need to break the repetitive reaction cycles that are part of our conditioning. We need the courage to create a space for a new experience with the issue.

You may find that Grace reveals the absurdity of the issue, and the misidentification becomes crystal clear. You may feel that the issue gets scarier, which will show you how much more you are attached to it then you were aware of. (Really valuable information.)

Or, you may realize that you could not sit with it without going to one of your old techniques or reactions. This will show you how conditioned you are. (More good information.)

If you are willing to consciously and consistently enter the unknown, with Grace as your guide, you will discover new fields of possibility, freedom and oneness.

Within what we call "consciousness" there appears to be two kinds of activity:

1. Everyday human thinking: reasoning, analyzing, the moment-by-moment mind chatter, knowledge, opinions, beliefs, judgments, concepts, etc.

2. The Kingdom of Heaven that is within us: deep yearnings for, and expressions of, wholeness and Oneness; intuitive clarity; unreasonable forgiveness; the presence of stillness; uncontrollable laughter; deep listening; bursts of creativity that feel like they arrived as a gift; Grace-driven actions; tangible abiding peace...

If we are hanging out day-by-day only in the first, we can tend to feel very busy, driven to get it all done (some how), and somewhat hollow...the "Is this all there is to life?" space.

When we dwell in the second, even for brief moments, there is a shift; a penetrating depth of resonance where borders and edges are transcended and we are quenched by Grace.

There is nothing wrong with #1. It works for a lot of our lives. But is will not give us #2.

#2 will include whatever we need for #1, with the additional bonus that a separate, limited sense of self diminishes as Oneness dawns.

Any thought that comes where you question your worth as a person, is 100% impersonal, completely unoriginal, and has come to every person on the planet. It is a homeless imposter, posing as your identity, and seeing it as such, is all you need to do.

How you showed up on the planet is how you showed up. It's just what is. It's not good or bad. Why did you show up this way? It doesn't matter. Any answer to that is a distraction the mind is posing. What's it going to do for you?

Just love that you get to be conscious in this moment, right now. And, you get to view your life as a classroom instead of a prison. Let Grace be your teacher, and enjoy the lessons! (There are no grades because no one is evaluating your progress.)

There is a common tendency in the human mind to believe that you can really mess up your life. It is based on the premise that you are in charge of yourself and that if you make "mistakes," or choices that you now see as not "wise," then you are stuck, or at least greatly hampered.

If you believe this, then you have bought into the conditioning of the dreaming mind. You can tell it is a dream because it may at times feel like a nightmare. This is a clear sign that you are asleep (which is actually great news!)

The key here is that Life has not given up on you! You have just temporarily dozed off and believed your limited thoughts. The result is you are having a limited experience. This is not permanent.

So if you find yourself in this condition, what can you do? Give up, and wake up.

Really, give it up. Clearly, believing whatever you have been believing, and thus doing, is not working. Identify those sleepy beliefs, assumptions and stories that say you are limited, and question them. See if they are really true.

Get as still as you can, and in humility, open up to Grace, and listen. Grace is always there and all it asks for is your attention (and not even that is a requirement).

You actually cannot be separate from the intelligent order of Life, any more than a tree can be separate from nature.

Imposters

You have never been
damaged or violated.
Lies don't change
what is real and true.
They just stand as impersonators
in the place of reality,
in a confused mind.

Ever notice how much we measure things, talk about them, and then have our level of happiness and peace determined by the numbers? We do this with age, size, weight, bank accounts, prices, temperature, days off, time, distance, miles per gallon, scores in sports, hours of sleep, compliments, Facebook "likes," etc.

Why do we let our contentment fluctuate with our fabricated numerical judgments? This story creation is just another game our conditioned mind plays to distract us from surrendering everything to Grace.

Have you noticed the mind's constant desire to need something (really everything) to be different than it is?

- "It's too cold!"
- "In December it should be much colder than this!"
- "Does it have to rain right when I'm going out?"
- "We need rain so badly, this is crazy."
- "I can't believe she said that! What's up with her?"
- "He knows I don't like to be late!"
- "I really need some new clothes."
- "Not that for dinner, again!"

This could go on endlessly (and it does).

Entertaining these thoughts does not impact one thing positively, and keeps us asleep.

How about just for one day, when this kind of thought arrives, instead of voicing it, just notice it, and let it rest? Are you in?

You can't control which thoughts come to you. Yet, you keep trying. Why? You want a sustained peaceful experience that looks and feels a very specific way, and you will pretty much do whatever it takes (including using spirituality) to get it.

The problem is, what you want is not possible. You can't control which thoughts come to you. They arise, they stay, they may go, they may come back. If you try to control them you will drain yourself, and go crazy. You can't have sustained human feelings, as much as your mind wants them. Chasing them is useless (even though we do this all the time).

Trying to control your thoughts is like trying to control the speed and direction of the wind. So, you won't feel peaceful until the wind stops gusting out of the North? And you pray to get it to stop. And then one morning it does. No wind. And Ahhhhh… Peace at last.

But wait, what was that you felt? You thought it stopped. Dang! There it is again.

What you can do is question if you need certain thoughts or experiences in order to be peaceful. Is that really true? Most likely you will find that where you are stuck is with your conditioned beliefs. Instead of believing you need something that changes to be in a permanent state to make you happy, just notice that belief. This sounds really simple, and it actually is.

When we notice and question our thoughts and feelings, vs. believing them, an entirely new phase of our existence appears. We enter a spacious field of Grace, free of willfulness and want.

Each situation, activity and interpersonal relationship in your day can be used to heighten your self-awareness. If something you experience triggers stress or anxiety, these feelings were already within you waiting to be released. But, you may not have been conscious of them.

Think of it this way. If your guitar is out of tune, when it has the experience of being plucked, it won't sound right. The outside activity triggers the awareness of a state within the guitar that already exists.

An appropriate response would not be to blame the hand that plucked the strings; it would be to bring the internal resonance into harmony with an agreed upon standard.

There is no judgment needed that this is a good or bad guitar, just gratitude that this experience has brought to consciousness the need for fine-tuning.

Spiritualized Egos

Watch out
for spending hours and days
on questions
that may help you clarify
some puzzling metaphysical concepts,
vs. those that help you
walk more tangibly
in judgment-free compassion
and hit-the-street unity.

The concepts
will keep you engaged
in your mind forever,
and all you end up with
is a spiritualized ego.

They may not make
a speck of difference
in how you treat your neighbor.

The reason the ego is so afraid is that when it looks in the mirror it sees nothing. Its full time job is to try to convince you that you need it, so it has an identity.

What if when you looked out at the world, you could only see a picture of what your mind has accepted as real and possible? In other words, you are watching a 3-D movie with surround sound, which your mind is projecting.

Let's slow this down, and really ponder some implications if this was true.

In this way, life would be mirroring back to you "on the outside," what your mind is consciously and unconsciously believing "on the inside."

This means that if you judge someone out there (in your movie), you are really judging your mind's limited story about them. If you don't like someone, then you don't like the way your mind made them up, and the beliefs your mind is holding about them. It is not really about them at all.

This might highlight the importance of:
    A. Realizing you are not your mind, and
    B. Becoming conscious of your mind's individual and collective beliefs, and unlearning or releasing those that are inconsistent with your deepest sense of Good.

Ever notice how when a feeling comes by that it is just a feeling? Once you perceive it, then you claim it as yours by using words like "I am sad. I am confused. I am happy. Etc."

A feeling is like a cloud. When a cloud comes by it is just a cloud. It is not your cloud. You don't think, "I am cumulous."

It is the mental activity that we call ego that has to grab things and make them ours. This gives the only supposed validity there is to a separate self or "me." Without attaching itself to something it has nothing, because it is nothing.

When you identify with a feeling, you then believe that you are that feeling. There is a separate "me" that is feeling something.

When the "me" is not attached to any thoughts or feelings, it fades and is replaced by you simply being the activity of one Life. This is your natural, ego-free, authentic self.

A paradox is something that appears self-contradictory, inconsistent, illogical, even impossible. When these appear the conditioned mind analyzes it hard. You can almost feel the gears grinding as it tries to squeeze meaning out of it.

If it can't make sense of it then it either judges and dismisses the statement, or judges and dismisses the person who made it (or both). All because it does not fit into its pre-determined logical framework for the way things are.

This kind of reasoning keeps us fearfully or self-righteously locked in a very narrow perspective of reality, and limits our insights to those that reinforce our current worldview.

The unconditioned mind seeks out and embraces paradoxes because it knows that it need not have anything figured out. It doesn't have cherished concepts to which it holds tightly. It leans completely into the unknown, intuitive flow of Grace.

It doesn't have a pre-determined, pre-conditioned framework. It wouldn't begin to imagine that it would try to put channel markers in the middle of the ocean!

It enjoys the space of discovery and embraces unlearning, even if its perceived sense of identity is on the line. Like a child, it remains open and trusts that it's a friendly universe.

Contemplating the Gift of Sky

The sky is.
Birds fly through the sky,
but the sky is not birds.

Clouds move through the sky,
but the sky is not clouds.
If it was,
when there are no clouds,
there would be no sky.

At night it appears to hold everything,
yet it appears as nothing.

The sky is like consciousness.
Thoughts move through it,
are even held by it,
but they don't become it.

By falsely identifying with thoughts and feelings
you may think that they are your consciousness.
This is because you are dreaming:
unconscious of your real consciousness.

No part of your eternal consciousness ever changes.
It is the all of I AM.
No part of you ever changes.
You are I AM expressed as all.

That which changes points you
either toward or away from Reality.

This moment's dictation
points me towards it.

So, let's pretend that there is this universal dream. And in this make believe dream world you think you are a seed. This dream has convinced you that you have been spit forth like a watermelon seed from a parent seed. It suggests that your life is surrounded by edges: that you are encased in limits on all sides.

It then some how stretches the now into a delusion called past and future, and gets you to be magnetically attracted to both ends of the continuum. Bizarre dream.

Next, it magically gets your shell to grow bigger and bigger, and then to maintain for a while, and then shrink back to smallness. Even more bizarre. Who thought this thing up?

And then it tells you that your life purpose is to gather (and keep) as much cool seed stuff as possible, on you and around you, so that you can attract other seeds to like you.

In the dream, it suggests that you ask questions about where the shell came from. In this way it tries to get you to think that being shell-like is the totality of all things real.

And then, ultimately, the dream gets you to leave your shell, and then it tells other seeds that they are supposed to feel sad and miss your shellness. I know, really strange.

Now, what if everything in this dream is the exact opposite of reality?

When you go outside the mind's habitual conditioning, you experience a freedom where self-consciousness effortlessly drops away. This has happened to all of us in some way. Picture a time when you were so in your zone that you weren't concerned about yourself, an outcome, others, or anything. You were totally in the burgeoning fullness of that moment.

This could have been gazing at a sunset, watching a bird soar, dancing, singing, writing, listening, playing a sport, acting…it goes on and on.

Life is filled with these moments. Can you remember what they feel like? Some may last only a few seconds, but each one points to experiencing Life without the filter where your ego tells you things needs to be different.

Living in these egoless moments more consistently is the entire point of unlearning. As you recognize and depersonalize the egoic patterns, they are released, and Reality is experienced throughout your day, as raw, unfettered, authentic grace.

Chapter 7

Relationships Grounded in Grace

Ever met someone that by the way they lived, you just naturally felt better about yourself whenever you were around them? And, they were not trying to have this impact on you.

When Grace permeates a life, you feel seen, embraced and uplifted in its presence.

You are not responsible for helping anyone change their behavior. You are responsible for how you see them, and for your response to their behavior no matter how they show up.

(Depending upon what you see and how you respond, you may help them more than you will ever know.)

As you mature in life, are you noticing your thought narrowing and constricting, or widening and releasing?

Are you noticing yourself doing more talking, or listening?

Are you noticing in conversations you are trying to convince, or accepting people's perspectives as valid for them?

Are you noticing that when you think of specific friends, colleagues, or family members, that you feel joined and united with them, or separate and distanced?

The first step to awakening to your oneness with all being in Life, is noticing how you are showing up. It's a big one.

While running on a beach, I once watched a pair of seagulls flying about five feet apart, soaring over the water, turning, gliding, flapping and staying that close the whole time. It was like a pas de deux in the air. Clearly they were communicating in some perfect way. They were listening to the same music.

What arrested my attention and inspired me was that apparently they had each mastered the art of individual flying. And, because they could both fly well, they then could accept the additional treat of communicating and having a relationship while flying! Each had found it's zone, stayed in it, and then this allowed for tandem soaring!

Are you interested in being in a relationship that soars into the unknown and reveals heavenly patterns of Grace? Instead of desperately wanting someone to inspire you with his or her soaring, take your soaring to the next level by leaving your self-grounding patterns of judgment, and glide on the thermals of unconditional acceptance.

This reveals the kind of music that the entire universe dances to!

Your Problem

If you have a problem
with someone else's behavior,
that is accurate.

You have made their behavior
your problem.

They have no ability
to make their behavior
your problem.

Only you can do that.

Wanting another to do anything so that you can feel a
certain way, is a sign of control and dependency.

When you are asleep there is no separation in your dream. Everything you experience is part of your consciousness, your projection, your dream. No matter how someone shows up, it is your dream. If you are disturbed in your dream by someone, you are disturbing yourself. You would not think of blaming another. It is your dream. This is not difficult to accept.

Ready for a leap?

When you are awake there is no separation in your awareness of the world. Everything you experience is part or your consciousness, your projection, your awareness of the world. No matter how someone shows up, it is your awareness of them you are experiencing. If you are disturbed in your awareness by someone, you are disturbing yourself. You would not think of blaming another. It is your awareness.

This may be more difficult to accept, but it is equally true, and, ultimately a huge step toward liberation.

If you want to feel a stillness and peace beyond your mind, consciously allow everything to be as it is. Try it. Accept, even for a few seconds, that nothing needs to change. Take a deep breath of that air. This reveals the foundation of unconditional love.

Is there anything anyone has done that has triggered in you a response to love them less? If so, you have just found the source of your pain. It is never their actions that cause you pain. It is your withholding of love. We are not built to obstruct love.

Ever notice how birds that fly by don't ask for your permission before they enter your awareness? Ever notice how friends and family that fly by don't ask for your permission before they enter your awareness?

We would never think of trying to control a bird, but can spend a whole lifetime trying to control our loved ones. It can take the form of wanting them to act a specific way so that you feel understood or loved.

Love that has to be earned is not worth a penny.

Invisible Rainbows of Grace

Ah,
how sweet
is the feeling
of having your all-consuming issue
completely enfolded and embraced
by the only Solution in the universe!

We are here
for each other
to be the surround-sound
of Soul.

Grace is the music
that comes from all directions
at once
and so permeates your senses
that the material is transmuted
without you even knowing it
and you find yourself
being sustained
in the reality of Love.

And then,
you are part of the music,
as you see your role
grow indescribably BIGGER
than the refrain
that has been stuck in your head
for what seems like forever.

The gift of Grace
meets you
as you
yearn and ask and move
out of the mortal echo,
into new stillness.

You are caught
as you
crescendo
from self-absorption
into the gentle up-draft
of Soul-absorption.

Invisible rainbows of Grace
sing you
a promise,
a covenant,
which expands you on purpose,
into the eternal harmonics of Life.

A ny activity that is based on separating from others through denying equality of rights, is completely short-sighted: whether personally or globally. It will eventually inflict suffering on the initiator, and if sustained, lead to its self-destruction. Ultimately our affections learn to embrace everyone. Oneness simply is All.

When you are unlearning, you begin to get very clear insights about what you are not. You realize that, even though these may have been unconscious, you have been acting them out for years. An example of this is believing you are not a "control freak," and then beginning to notice how much you:

- Try to influence others impressions of you
- Avoid authentic conversations
- Get worried when things don't go as planned
- Steer clear of feedback from others
- Get upset with others if their behavior does not match your desires
- Try to get others to do what you want them to do
- Avoid discomfort (even when it involves accomplishing an important goal)
- Tell half-truths
- Exaggerate
- Fret over the amount of money in your bank account
- Treat others in a way that they will love you so you can feel worthy
- Need to know how things will work out in your career, relationships, etc.
- Accept the status quo, so you won't ruffle any edges
- Continually try to predict the future
- Need life to be different than it is right now
- Don't trust the unknown, so you do everything you can to avoid surprises

Just to name a few…

One Heart

Our hearts are connected
no matter what our head says.

Can you find someone
with whom you don't feel close?

Now find
the part of your heart
that has even a little
compassion for them.
That space of tenderness
is in there,
because your heart
does not exist by itself.
It is the extension
of the one heart
that is Love.

Once you find it,
hold them in close.
Be in that feeling.

Joining brings softening.
Separation maintains hardness.

Have your ever heard someone's deepest, heartfelt conviction about the nature of reality, and thought that they, and those in that tradition, just don't get it? And then you may have likely wished that if they only knew what you know, then they would see the light.

If they left the conversation with the same well-intentioned mindset as you, then you have both judgmentally reinforced the ego's way it fractures life into me and mine vs. you and yours. This is, and will, produce tension, war, and suffering, while it is held onto.

As long as you see anyone you meet as needing to be different in order to be at one with Truth, you will perpetuate duplicity and separation. The door way into the Kingdom of Heaven is through seeing everyone as already there.

Whatever you think you need from someone, must first be found within, and given to yourself and others. When you are full, your needs diminish, and Oneness emerges.

Is there a point in your experience with another that you decide they should know better? For example, we tend to think that when children are really young, they may not have learned enough to know better. How much learning is enough? If you raised children, was there a time when you shifted into this mindset?

With a sibling or partner, has there come a point where you think the other should know better (like when they have not met an expectation you or others had for them)?

If you can remember when you began this judgment, what do you think it communicated to them? Is it still communicating something to them?

We can never possibly know why someone does what he or she does. They may not know why they do most of what they do. If we are honest, we don't know why we do much of what we do: habits, conditioning, patterns, education, muscle memory, motives, yearnings, and on and on. It is actually all irrelevant. It is what it is.

Can you let all that go (please), and be with another as if today was the only time you ever got to be with them? If this moment was all you had, how would you show up? What would really matter? As you yield into this space of humble stillness, Grace will form your words and actions... This will be enough.

Ouch!

If you knew
that where everyone is
right now
in the unfoldment of their identity
is exactly where they need to be
in their path to awaken,
would you still want them
to be different for you?

When you see and love the potential in another, can you also cherish them at the same time as they are right now, humanly (the whole package)?

If you sense that you are focusing more on their potential than where they are right now, then this is likely felt by them, and will come across as conditional love. You may want to check it out, because sometimes when we hold tightly to a spiritual view of another, we focus so much on that, that they don't feel we love them as they think they are humanly right now. This can be a very lonely place.

Bonus section for the authentically-hearted: If you are not sure how you are coming across, and you really want to know, you might ask them: "Can you tell (and feel) that I love you exactly as you are, and also that I see in you, all you can become?" You may already know the answer, so you may not need to ask it. But if you are not sure, you could ask. If you get an honest answer, it could be very revealing, no matter what it is.

Starting with Me

Why do I yearn
to be understood,
and get so upset
when I am misunderstood,
since when I really look at it,
I don't even understand myself?

When you have been misunderstood and misrepresented, can you move through it untouched?

Can you love that the person is doing what they feel is right, and bless them on their path?

It has nothing to do with you or anyone else. Their words and actions tell you about them. Period. They are doing their best, just as we all are.

There is nothing to defend because there has been no crime. Your response tells you about yourself. Can you take in what has been said, consider it humbly, use what Grace tells you to use, release the rest, and move on?

When was the last time you tried to change someone, or wished they were different than they are? When was the last time you voiced this desire to a third person?

When someone doesn't act the way you think they should, you are abiding in judgment. You may then find yourself feeling anxious, frustrated, disappointed, upset, or resentful. It may even be well meaning and disguised as, "It would help them so much if they would only _____! Or, "Why don't they just_____?"

The more you focus on altering someone (anyone), the more it distracts you from being your authentic Self. As you awaken beyond your limited conditioning, any effort to try to change somebody begins to lose interest to you.

Today, they are as they are. Simple fact. It does not mean they don't have potential. It does not mean they are not whole and complete: at one with Love. It simply means that you are not in charge of how and when they evolve.

Have you found the freedom and deep joy of celebrating people independent of how they show up? This is loving another without conditions. You can't fake this.

It can change everything.

Each of us plays many roles like: parent, teacher, friend, leader, family member, etc. In these roles, if people ask you for help, you have two blueprints from which you can assist them:

1. They are a being that needs something they are lacking. Or,
2. They are the consciousness of the One Being and include whatever they think they need.

One or the other of these models is always in your thought, and is communicated to the other.

In the first approach you will feel responsible for helping them get better. In the second approach you will feel the freedom to celebrate their immaculate wholeness and watch Grace unfold the interaction.

If you are teaching spirituality, your approach brings people into relationship with what you think is most important. What is most important to you? Here are a few options:

- Are you teaching children, students, even each other, that what matters most is developing their relationship with specific behaviors and spiritual practices? For most youth (and adults), this approach creates a disconnect which never brings them into an experiential relationship with God.

- Or, are you teaching people that what matters most is to learn about metaphysics, in hopes that they will some day learn how to apply it? This approach can feel abstract and dry, and often wilts in the head.

- Or, are you teaching people that what matters most is developing one's authentic, pragmatic, affectionate relationship with the Divine, in whatever ways are most meaningful to them? Here, the presence of Oneness is awakened.

What would those you are influencing say you are emphasizing?

What are you emphasizing in your own spiritual education?

How do we help our children (and students) navigate the waters of duality and awaken to Oneness?

We can't do it for them. But, we can do it for ourselves. And, as long as we are with them, we can model this supreme gift.

Here are some models for learning and teaching that embrace children as well as adults:

- First and foremost it is about "Seeing." What we see is more important that what we say. See each as whole and complete. If you see them as needing your help, then you are caught in the dream of separation.

- Learning requires a willingness to face transformation: to go beyond our current form of thinking and embrace the Unknown. Are we modeling this for our children in transparent ways? Do they see us leaving the old for the new? Do we model self-forgiveness? Do we make amends with them if we realize we would now do something different than we did? Do we listen to, and follow, Grace?

- Teaching involves providing a space where others can experience, discover, and practice, truth. Do we provide experiences where they can discover what works for them? Do we not solve all their problems? Do we help them learn to listen to what is their "truth" vs. ours? Do we really listen curiously to what is true for them, without trying to lead them somewhere?

For sure there is much more, but this foundation could be quite a gift.

Each of us has an "Inner Teacher" that is governing us 24/7. But, we may never have learned how to be in consistent, conscious, contact with this Guiding Presence. Nevertheless, it is there, waiting to be listened to.

What if, instead of trying to offer solutions to each other's problems, our focus as a helping friend, teacher, parent, or spouse, was to listen in a way that helped our friend hear his/her Inner Teacher? What a gift!

M any of us find it hard to love ourselves. This often comes from one ingrained thought: You believe that you should be different than you are.

This thought may be conditioned in your mind because:
1. You have a standard you are holding up, and believe you should be at this standard. Or,
2. You compare yourself to others, and believe you should be as good or better than them.

All this is thinking that instills suffering. And it should, because it is based in judgment and separation, and is delusionary reasoning. In this moment, how can you be different than you are? Where you are right now is where you are. It's not good or bad, it's just where you are.

We are used to judging, and then deciding if we will love what we have judged. What's up with that craziness? How about dropping the judging part, and just love?

If you are waiting for someone to change so that you can really love them, what if they never change? Could mean you will never love them. Ouch. Separation.

The love that is based on the fulfillment of specific conditions is not love. It is positional affection.

What if instead, you loved them without needing them to change? Could mean you will always love them. Yup. Oneness.

In every relationship it is one or the other.

When I choose to love you regardless of how you act, I am free.

Relationships Grounded in Grace

Chapter 8

Communicating from Oneness

Have you ever been seen by someone with eyes that are incapable of judging you? They see who you are, sometimes clearer than you do. You could tell them the worst thing you have ever done, and their view of you would not budge. They don't confuse who you are, with what you have done.

When these people listen to you, you find new spaces emerging in you, where you catch glimpses of what they are seeing, and realize it has been there all along. Their eyes become your eyes, and you share a common heart.

We are made to be this gift of Grace for each other.

Instead of thinking of yourself as someone who helps other people, how about starting from the premise that those you are with are whole and complete, and are not in need of your help?

Can you view anyone you're with as needing nothing from you? This doesn't mean you won't love them. But, as you join them in equality, it could entirely shift the way in which you see and interact with them.

When communicating with someone, whether through face-to-face, phone or in writing, let's pause… and open our receptive faculties to what is authentically being born that moment.

It is through this kind of fresh listening that you can penetrate the veil of stagnation and let Grace land. You are new each moment, and so is every communication you will ever receive or send. There is no repetition.

Let's start to build silences right into the middle of our conversations. And in that sacred space we can listen for what needs to be heard.

Can you "hold the space" in a conversation?

Can you be completely present, and give the other person room to pause and reflect? When you ask a question, can you let the other person think about their response without offering any guiding remarks or possible answers to choose from?

When they respond, can you actually ask a second question based on their response? This is so unusual. And, rarest of all, possibly a third one? And can you have no intentions in these questions to get them to see anything your way?

Can you pull in beside the other person in a way that you are not guiding the conversation in the slightest: zero, zip, not even with your facial expression or tone? Can you walk with them in the woods and let them completely choose where you go?

This could feel a little awkward at first, because neither of you may be used to it.

I'm not suggesting you always do this. But I am offering it as an option that could reveal a hidden treasure chest of pure gems within each of you. It can also take any relationship to an entirely authentic place: the ever-fresh pasture of Grace.

The next Insight will open up more about this gift you can practice with anyone, regardless of their age or stage of maturity…

Learning to naturally "hold the space" in a conversation with others, begins with how you see and hold the space for yourself. If this is important to you, then you already may be devoted to solo dancing with Grace.

Each day you know that if nothing else happens, you will have moments consecrated to listening and responding to your Inner Choreographer.

As you enter this sacred studio, you accept with reverence, that you are a blessed vehicle where Grace reveals and expresses natural beauty. You see yourself and others through pure, lucid, unlimited eyes. Wherever you look you see Oneness, not duplicitous gaps and needs.

The natural light of Self-realization illuminates your consciousness as you listen and feel the improvisational movement of Soul. No predictions, just complete, joyous openness to any possibility.

By practicing listening each day in this holy space, when you get to pas-de-deux, you naturally trust Grace to reveal how and when you listen and speak. The communication activities identified in the previous Insight can be a natural outcome of how Grace dances as us.

A Landing Strip for Angels

Conflict is a battle,
disagreement,
or mental struggle.

What if you were to meet conflict
solely with Grace-impelled observation?
In that moment
there would be no conflict,
just one side
presenting a point of view,
and you gently noticing.

Perhaps
dwelling in humble stillness
would reveal the manger
in which you can listen
to what is being offered,
and see if there is a message in it
that you need to hear right now.

This graceful consideration
can provide
a landing strip for angels
that reawaken you
to your common Heart.

What do you do when someone you love is deeply confused? Do you battle their confusion by trying to straighten them out? How effective has this been?

How about joining with them? How do you do this?

You listen:
- You pull in beside them as if they were driving, and let them take you where they want to go.
- You let them drive, without trying to grab the wheel.
- As they describe the scenery from their perspective, you tell them what you see in their scenery without adding any bias or interpretation.
- If you don't understand something they describe, you ask a question to clarify, but not to probe.
- If they ask you a question, you respond authentically.
- You find the parts of them that are clear, and you celebrate that.
- You trust that Grace is leading you both. Always.

Your mind will tell you this is not enough. You must fix them: get them back on the "right" path.

Your heart is so full accepting them, you feel no anxiety for them needing to change. Life is the path. Grace is within us all.

Next time you are listening to someone and you don't know what to say that may be helpful, shift from thinking about what to say, to seeing yourself and the other as whole and complete: at one with Life.

Hover with them in your non-judgmental heart, and silently drink from Truth, like a hummingbird gathering nectar from a flower. This may be for a moment, or many moments. Stay humbly quiet, seeing and listening, until Grace lifts you to speak or act.

You can trust that the giving and receiving are guided by your mutual Source.

Free at Last

There is deep freedom
in not needing to change
anyone's opinion
about anything.

How do you respond when you are offered unrequested feedback, a correction, suggestion, advice or criticism?

What if the first word out of your mouth was a genuine, "Thank you"? And then you honestly considered the offering to see if you could find any truth in it for you.

Their idea has entered your experience for a reason. If it came to your attention, why not see if there is a message in it from Grace. If there is, great! If not, great! Either way, you can go through the experience, and not carry it with you.

If someone gives you feedback you don't want to hear, it's like they are waking you up while you are sleeping, and telling you they believe the building is on fire. Instead of being grateful for the warning, because they are trying to save you immense suffering, what do you do?

- You get upset with the person for disturbing your peace.
- You tell them they are wrong.
- You judge them.
- You sit there and pray that that person will change their mind.
- You run from the person.
- You tell a friend how wrong the person is for giving you this feedback in hopes they will agree with you.
- You go hide in another room, in your cave.

Instead: how about humbly listening to their feedback, no matter how bizarre it seems, and seeing if it rings true at all? Their entire reason for being in your experience in this way, at this time, is to help you wake up. What a blessing!

When in a conversation, if you find yourself about to strongly defend your perspective, see if you can realize that someone else's outlook is just as valid as yours, even if you heard yours directly from God. They may feel the same way.

Bring your conviction into the silence and stillness that is beyond needing to be right, and sit there with it. See what happens if you don't lurch.

Feel what occurs when you are willing to release your issue to Grace, with no attachment to the outcome…and just listen: to them, to God, to this one Song singing you both forth. If you are inspired to speak at this point, Soul will form your words.

When you leave a conversation that did not go as you hoped, do you ever find yourself miffed because they did not understand you?

Often what masquerades as not being understood, is that they did not agree with you. We want our point of view confirmed. We want to be right.

The ego tells you that you need to be right: that your identity is the ideas and values you hold dearly. If your cherished concepts are not correct, then there is something wrong with you. So when someone does not understand you, with egoic reasoning, you feel wrong, devalued, even worthless. Yikes!

Let's give it a break. If you believe that someone did not get your point, then perhaps they did not get your point. That could be all of it. Or, possibly they did get your point, but did not agree. That's fine too.

Let's notice what we start to believe about others or ourselves in response to how they communicate with us. If we don't like the conclusions we have drawn, then we can question their veracity, versus cascading into judgment.

When someone asks us to help them with a problem, our tendency is to prepare by trying to figure out what they want to talk about, and how we may answer them.

How about trying the exact opposite process? Prepare by emptying your mind of any possible preconceptions about what you might say to them. Then, see the two of you as having access to the same infinite pool of Intelligence, and let this Ordering Presence lead the way.

When you leap into the unknown in this way, you can surrender to, listen to, and receive Grace. After all, they were really asking for help from Grace, and what you get to do, is get out of the way so that there is a space where this happens.

Two Dancing Butterflies

There is a way to listen
where a conversation
becomes an improvisational dance
in which all you are doing
is yielding
and responding to Grace.

It is not possible
for the conversation
to "take a wrong turn"
because there is no attachment
to controlling, directing,
guiding or influencing
the direction or outcome.

This does not take
the heavy lifting of concentration
to keep your mind focused.
Rather,
it is a releasing
where you are so at one with
the musical flow
of the unfolding dialogue
that there is nothing else going on.

No future.
No past.

Just the sacred space
of two dancing butterflies
connecting through awareness,
while responding
to your instinctual divine pattern,
as moved by Mother Nature.

There is a way to naturally listen to someone and God at the same time. In this dimension of communication, you tangibly feel the intimate presence of Grace, and your oneness with another. Doing this consistently and effectively requires an affirmative answer to the following question:

Are you learning to listen deeply to another, without any agenda, and practicing this often?

If your response is "No," you are likely too caught up in yourself and the drama in your or another's life. There may be too much self in the way. You may need to let go of even your well-intentioned desires to "help" another, and realize that you are not anyone's rescuer or savior.

If your response to the question is "Yes," and you have really experienced this, then you will find growing within you the yearning to bring an even deeper listening to them, beyond the personal. This humble longing is the door to learning to listen to the Divine.

If you want to experience the intimate presence of Grace and your oneness with another, more than anything else, you will find this natural capacity, through the discipline and humility to practice listening: first to another, then to God, then to both as one.

Three Approaches to Conversations

Attachment:
You are attached to needing the topic to be one in which you feel comfortable. If you find the topic offensive or unacceptable to your mental models, you try to change the topic, or just don't ask questions. Once you do this you feel peaceful. You are communicating to the person that you have no interest in their topic, or them.

Detachment:
When you find the topic of the conversation offensive or unacceptable to your mental models, you work hard to continually detach what the person is saying from who they really are, or from your view or what is real and true. Once you do this you feel peaceful. You are not really engaged in the conversation at a meaningful level. They may feel your distancing.

Non-Attachment:
There are no topics that are offensive or unacceptable to you. You are completely without agenda. Your view of life has already been anchored in Oneness before the conversation began. You are at peace. Period. Whatever topic they would like to open up is fine. You pull in beside them and really listen to them with your unselfed heart. You both feel connected in the presence of Grace.

People do not hear exactly what you say. They hear what they are ready and able to hear. After you speak with another, they are left with their interpretation of, or story about, what you said. Period.

Can you be completely OK with this, and let the conversation go? Or, are you attached to them needing to "get" you in the way you hoped for?

With young children we give them the space to make our words mean what they will. As they get older we may start to insist they get our perspective. When they don't, we may feel frustrated and think they should know better. Yikes! Who put us in charge of their interpretation of reality?

When this egocentric mindset is carried into adulthood, we isolate others and ourselves through continually judging them for not getting our meaning. And yet, we deeply yearn to feel more connected to, and intimate with, others. Something is off with this picture.

When you are in a situation where someone has asked for assistance, the motivation may arise: "I need to get this right for her."

This seems like a harmless enough thought. But, if it is left unquestioned it can actually disrupt the effort and outcome of whatever you are trying to do.

When you bring it to inquiry here are some questions that arise:
- How do I know what is right for her?
- Am I really just trying to get it right for me?
- Is it possible that if I got this wrong it could still bring about huge blessings (for her and me)?
- Is it possible to get it wrong?
- Am I trying to pre-determine what will happen?
- Do I feel pressure to control what happens to get it right?
- Who made me God?

Alternative Motivation: "I will act as Grace leads me. Each moment."

Do you ever feel somewhat awkward when you receive a deeply genuine compliment from someone? If so, here's an approach:

See if you can you find the place in you that authentically accepts and appreciates their praise, and at the same time, feels and knows that that which they are appreciating in you, they also have the capacity to express.

If you know that you come from a common Source, then you will receive the compliment as an acknowledgment of Grace. And, your verbal or written response will flow from this natural, spiritual affection, and will embrace the giver and all mankind.

When someone verbally attacks you, it does not mean they don't love you. It just means they are a little confused right now. If they were self-aware and trying to state it accurately, it might sound something like:

"Given the untrue thoughts I am believing about you and me right now, I am feeling insecure, and am finding it hard to face these feelings and question these beliefs. That's why I am pretending that you are the source of my pain.

"By taking out my stress on you, I don't have to address my beliefs, and I can continue to live under the delusion that I am OK, and just a helpless victim.

"I am treating you in this bazaar way to motivate you to stop what you are doing. If you act exactly as I would like you to act, I will have the momentary feeling of being in control. This will protect my fragile self-image, and thus I will feel better about myself.

"Please forgive me, but this is the best I can do right now."

The difference between something you believe vs. what you know for sure, is that when your beliefs are challenged it can upset you, and you likely feel the need to defend yourself. When something you know all the way from the center of your being is challenged, you just smile gently and have nothing to defend.

It simply does not matter what they say, because your knowing is anchored in your deepest truth. You can still listen and learn about their perspective, but whatever they say cannot threaten your peace. Living from the stillness of this kind of knowing is a gift to each of us from Grace.

Chapter 9

Living from Stillness

When you create a space to be deeply still in nature, really listening, feeling its message for you in this moment, something settles and adjusts. In this manger of sweet release, a gentle oneness emerges.

This may not happen when you just look at it briefly and think how beautiful it is. This may not get beyond the mind. It requires a conscious pause, a breathing in, an embracing acceptance of the presence that is our common Substance.

•

Next time you are feeling burdened, see if you can take a brief time out: a little huddle with Grace.

In that space, just notice the burdened feeling. During this moment of noticing, you won't feel burdened. You can't because awareness has no will, no expectation, no past to project into the future, no heaviness. In these few seconds you are experiencing your true divine essence: your authentic Self, your oneness with Life.

Sometimes this is enough to remind you of your Grace-driven nature, and the heaviness starts to evaporate. The windows are defogging and you can see clearly again. You may catch a glimpse that who you are cannot be burdened. It's just your misconception of yourself that you are believing in that can feel confused and overwhelmed.

I try to take several of these brief Grace-huddles each day. It is remarkably refreshing and really keeps things in perspective.

The point of a Grace-huddle mentioned in the previous Insight is to bring you into direct experience with the Divine.

In this sacred space, you are not in charge. You are not informing God about anything. You are not ruminating on issues in your life. You are not trying to fit divine revelation into your pre-conceived expectations.

You are opening in stillness and humbly listening. You are willing to act on what you hear, and keep listening. You are learning what the guiding presence of Grace feels like and realizing it is your constant companion.

It is from this poised, awake awareness(through noticing), and interaction(through listening), that you increasingly experience yourself as the freedom of Life!

Settling into Stillness

Give yourself the gift
each day,
of settling into Stillness.
Feel into One.

Allow any
border, wall, judgment, competition, or division,
to simply rest.
Let them be reconciled by Grace.
Each of these is just a grain of sand,
swirling
in the stream of consciousness.
Watch them settle to the earth
before you hit rock bottom.

This releasing
allows the Light to penetrate,
and for you to see
into deeper realms.
The depth was always there,
but with all the mental commotion,
you often didn't fathom
your own wisdom,
or see into the beauty of others.

In this Stillness
your non-attached clarity
embraces each solitude,
revealing us all
as the sacred community of Love.

We tend to live almost entirely in our minds, refereeing our moment-by-moment experience, blowing the whistle on anything that does not fit our pre-determined beliefs and standards. This can be exhausting and debilitating as we play out the role of non-stop air-traffic controller.

Enter: heart space.

Become so quiet, so still, so open to the all-inclusive oneness of Love, that the mind's compulsive contraction around objects, situations, and people starts to fade. What is released is a divinely sweet, natural, affection that is free of distinction and judgment. When you experience the uniting presence of condition-free acceptance, a new reality emerges that feels unmistakably real.

Grace exists so that you never again feel lonely or abandoned. It permeates our affections by releasing anything in us that separates us from others and Life. It guides us through stillness to feel and love that we really are all One.

Grace reveals a presence that has no opposites. This presence is your indestructible, authentic Self.

When Grace makes you aware of how the dreaming self operates, you begin to see that its cycles and patterns are completely impersonal. They simply are not you, any more than your current address is you. Both may be where you hangout and often return to, but they are not you. You are not a location or a mindset, no matter how often you frequent them.

You are the consciousness that has no borders, attachments, limits, judgments nor fixed opinions. And, you can at the same time, right now, live at an address; with things you like; with things you are not able to do; with a sense of what is right or wrong for you; and with preferences.

When you allow Grace to dance you, this incarnation becomes the stage to which you bring an unlimited freedom, brightness, and ego-free clarity. And what happens as we watch you? We are touched by the affectional presence of "All is well." You show us that our infinite nature is not confined by anything, anyone, or any place. Ever.

Thanks for the gift!

Receiving Gifts

Anything that disturbs your peace is a gift.
Are you ready to receive it?
It has arrived right on time
so that it can be unlearned.
It shows you where you are not free,
and invites you to liberation!

Of course,
you don't have to accept the disturbance
as a gift to awaken
to your ineffable wholeness and beauty.
You can fight it and push it away.
But, since it has no place to go
but to reside in your consciousness,
you will unconsciously
carry the disturbance with you.
It can ultimately weigh you down:
blurring your perceptions,
disrupting your actions,
and diminishing your results.

But it's never too late
to accept your gift.
The field of self-realization
is always ripe for harvest.

When you are ready,
go to the part of you
that doesn't have it all figured out.
Grace responds more eagerly
to humility than egocentricity.

It's hard to unwrap a gift
with your heart closed
and your hands in fists,
tightly grasping the known.

Open
your mind and heart and palms
to your authentic Self:
the unlimited divinity
in you and everyone.
Stand there in stillness,
available to the infinite Field of Love:
the Kingdom of Heaven within.
Feel the transcendent embrace
as you let yourself
and everyone
be owned by Love.

As you go through your day, when you become aware of situations happening in the world, can you see them simply as information being offered to you in a collective movie?

See if you can avoid jumping into its worldview and forming an opinion about it, judging it, personalizing it, and shoulding all over it? It is just an invitation you can notice: an impersonal perspective using people to broadcast itself.

You are an individual divine consciousness that can notice any information without believing it or taking it in, even if it has your or another's name on it. When you see through these non-judging eyes, you will experience the clarity to know what is true or not. You won't be ignorantly tricked to react. This sacred clarity frees your actions to flow from Grace.

When Grace drives actions, it reveals the experience of loving beyond your conditioning, or unconditional love.

A dualistic consciousness tends to divide, separate, categorize, and compartmentalize in an effort to maintain its identity and specialness. It feels the need to figure everything out, achieve something, and sustain an ideal.

A unified consciousness notices, listens, joins, merges, and makes connections. It has no needs that drive it because is sees all as One. It is delighted to explore, unlearn and discover.

If someone says or does something that bothers you, in a dualistic mindset there is an automatic tendency to judge or blame.

From a unified mindset you are aware that if something bothers you, it must be in your consciousness. So you take a gentle glance at your own landscape to see where you can find the issue within you.

Here are some examples as we transition from a dualistic to a unified awareness:

"He should not be so abrupt!" becomes "Am I being abrupt any where in my life right now?"

"She needs to know when to stop talking so much!" becomes "Where do I need to stop talking so much, to others, or in my self-talk?"

"That government should stop the oppression!" becomes "Where in my life am I oppressing or coercing others, or myself?"

In each example, listen in stillness, let Grace guide you, and see if can you find it.

What Changed?

Here you are at peace,
just being…

The next moment
a thought enters,
you choose to believe it,
and now you are worrying.
Really?

Did your peaceful being leave,
or did you just choose
to identify with
a passing thought?

There is a tendency to think that life is happening TO US. We can feel like abandoned victims.

As we progress we transition to believing that life is happening FOR US. We can still feel separate, but blessed by life.

Finally, we recognize that Life is happening AS US. We and Life are one. We already include every thing we ever thought we needed.

When you are listening to God and you hear nothing, you are witnessing unmanifested Divine potential. The Divine is still there, it's just not showing up in the way your mind expects it to.

The ego thinks this is a void, calls it nothing, and quits listening. Staying in stillness, with the yet to be revealed, is your next frontier. What an adventure!

Watching in Awe

When you demand nothing
from the moment,
you are releasing
your fabricated role
as the source of anything.
It is not up to you
to change the world
(or even your world).

In this moment
you can realize
that the presence of Grace
is enough,
and then adopt
an appreciative consciousness:
watching in awe
as Life unfolds
without your contriving.

Stillness is a space of Grace that is always there within you. You don't concentrate your way into stillness. It is not something you try to do. It doesn't take time or the right conditions to experience this precious space of resonating silence.

It is something you release into. Something that you allow to emerge.

As you let each little and big concern go, you find Stillness surrounding you. You can rest in it, and trust its Mothering presence.

Listening is not thinking about what you will say as soon as someone is done talking. It is being so completely involved in the unfolding moment that your are naturally yielding to when to pause and when to speak.

Stillness is vital to this sense of presence. When you show up coming from a place of deep inner stillness, you don't try to control the conversation. You let it be revealed as a dance that Grace is choreographing between the two of you.

Would you like to feel more divine Oneness and Presence? Do you think this will come through speaking, or listening, to God?

When you are praying you may find that you are doing all the talking. You may not recognize it as talking. You may think of it as reinforcing in your mind what is real and true in order to receive an intended outcome. Here your effort may be put into forming the right words and concepts so as to offer the right argument or affirmation.

The mind likes this kind of prayer because it feels in control. It does not go into the Unknown, so it feels safe in its own little world. Praying in this manner may never leave your mind. Not much divine presence there.

Instead how about yielding your desires to God from the very beginning? How about letting Grace impart what is needed? Here your effort is put into surrendering all issues to Truth, and listening with all your heart. This approach is scary for the mind because it requires leaving the known, and trusting in, and listening to, the Unknown.

When you really listen to the Divine, you may hear and feel the sound of gentle stillness, the Inner Teacher. And, you may feel the connection of your coexistence with Love.

Being stillness

You walk silently
into a green and golden field,
sprinkled with bushes,
and edged with dark green woods.
The only sound
is the barely audible wind,
and the melody of birds chirping.
You sit in tranquility,
allowing your expanding embrace
to breathe it all in,
with awe.

Nothing needs to be analyzed
or understood.
You let what enters the field
move where it moves.
You are still.

You don't try to move closer to anything
so that you can see and remember it.
You don't try to gather anything
so you can store it,
and use it as a keepsake or reminder.

You are at one with Nature,
simply living in this moment
of your burgeoning awareness of Being.

Being stillness.

What if this was your model for prayer?

There is a tendency in the human mind to think that good comes to you from outside you. If you believe this, you may find yourself doing a lot of wishing and hoping and waiting. You may feel separated from good at times.

With this line of reasoning, when good does come to you, you may feel like this divine Something, for some reason, finally blessed you. There is a feeling of two: you working things out, and the good Source.

Alternatively, you can realize that good comes from within you. In the same way as the fruit on a tree does not come from outside it, it comes from within it as an expression of nature. All good comes from within you because you are the expression of the Divine.

If you begin from the premise that you already include all good, then you can trust that Nature will ripen your fruit in the time and space needed. You don't try to speed it up; you yield to and express this perfect Intelligence.

While it can feel seasonal, when you realize that in Consciousness all seasons are happening simultaneously, then there is always fruit ready for harvest.

Let Grace Land

In the presence of Grace
you experience
that which words
cannot reach.
It is that which is
beyond what the mind can grasp...

It is the experience
that does not arrive
because you did something...

It emerges more
from what you did not do.

Just be still,
Give up trying to think
the perfect truth,
or to be perfect.

Just let grace land...

Chapter 10

Embracing
the Darkness

There is a divine order for your life, no matter what you are going through.

If you don't see it in the moment, that does not mean it does not exist. It's your perception that is off, not the order.

When an unexpected difficult event occurs, our thought naturally goes to "Why did this happen?" If the answer is not immediately obvious, watch out for the tendency to dwell there and ruminate endlessly.

The mind loves to get distracted in the "Why" world. It likes to put a specific cause to something, and then judge that cause, often creating perpetrators and victims. This is not a healthy place.

Instead: Ask Grace, "What do I need to see right now?" Then listen and take notes.

Imagine if you spent the hours, days, weeks, months (and even years), listening to Grace whenever the topic came up, vs. searching within the walls of your conditioned mind. It's like we think we are going to get something better from continual analysis than listening to Grace. I don't think so.

Trust Grace to show you what you need to know.

Entanglement in any form is here to show you what you are not.

Dominion will not come in the future. It is now or never.

Truth doesn't have a future tense. It gives you everything right now. It is all yours for the accepting.

One way to view life is that you are a separate being like a tree is a separate being. Another way to view life is that you are being lived by Life, like a tree is being lived by Nature.

If you identify with the separate view, you are likely trying in vain to control your life to make it what you want it to be. If you identify with being lived by Life, you are consciously surrendering your will to be the natural activity of Love.

Each of us is waking up from this dream of separation at the rate we are ready to. You could not have gone faster than you have, so there is no use looking back at anything with regret. The "If only I had..." Or, "Why didn't I..." are endless dead ends.

If you are finding a tendency to look back and feel disappointed, you might ask yourself what you are trying to accomplish through dwelling in your rearview mirror feelings. Disappointment and regret lead to discouragement and self-condemnation. This is not a healthy path, and not one that helps you consciously wake up now.

Can you find the part of you that is relentlessly graceful, unstoppably peaceful, authentically present, and prone to laugh?

No matter what is going on, there is a room in your house where this is alive right now. Your yearning and grateful heart is the doorway in.

The key to awakening from a dream is to start from where you are right now. You don't awaken in the past or the future. If you have turned away from yourself in a bad experience, the Self, who you really are, was never touched.

Go to the uncomfortable edge of the unknown that you ran from in your fear, and that you are still consciously or unconsciously avoiding. Stay there, as Grace carries you through the edge of your belief in a separate, scared self, and discover the freedom of what You are. You are That I AM.

Just because in your day-to-day life you may not be experiencing abundance right now, it does not mean you are deficient. To believe this would be like thinking that being in a cold breeze has something to do with how warm and caring a person you are.

Your experience is not an indicator of your worth. Ever!

Dealing With Darkness

I tried to do it alone.
I thought this was what you were supposed to do.

I strained to work it out on my own.
I gave it my best spiritual shot:
for hours at a time,
day after day,
for decades ...
But this did not work.

But still,
I knew I had to keep trying:
that somehow if I would shine the Light
on the darkness out there,
all would be well.

There was a lifetime of ignoring the darkness in here.
Oh, when cornered,
I would briefly shine my metaphysical flashlight into my void,
because I had too.
But all I found were self-sabotaged quick fixes
that turned me back to everyone else's darkness.

It was not until I could live the lie no longer
that I stepped into my own authentic, still-forming truth.

These were slow, brutal steps, that made no sense to some.
The kind where you feel punched-in-the-gut each morning.
These were willing-to-lose-it-all steps.
But they were impelled.

Most of the time I could only hear one thing:
"Just keep walking and stay open ..."
Destination, irrelevant!

Then one morning after months of walking
and a very long silence,
I heard Grace ask:
"What's the point of it all? Really.
What do you want in life more than anything?"

The answer was instant
and felt righter than anything, ever.
"To learn to love without judgment."
That's all I really want!

And with it I knew where Grace was leading me:
"Now you are going to walk into and embrace your darkness,
because that is where
you are guaranteed to learn to love without judgment.
And once you are in that darkness you get to,
listen,
and unlearn,
and thus love without judgment.
Over and over and over ..."

And, so that's where I am today.
Still walking, into the darkness.
But not alone.
And with an illumined peace
that is beyond words.

When we are shocked by a tragedy, it can understandably feel like it shakes our whole world. Of course we respond in deep brotherly and sisterly love and compassion in whatever way we are led by Grace.

Many of us are struggling with how to process these events. The following is offered as an approach that may be helpful.

In any situation we ultimately have a choice about where we allow ourselves to dwell:

- Truth
- The human facts
- Your story

Truth: One infinite Being. One Consciousness. One Life, in which there is no death.
The human facts: Whatever happens on the human stage. Everything comes and goes. Nothing is permanent.
Your story: Whatever you believe about the facts while ignoring Truth.

You don't ignore the facts. This happened in accord with how things work on the human scene. You just notice it, without getting caught in it. This is what can happen in dreams.

You also notice your stories, or what you are making the events mean for yourself and others. You will not be at peace as long as you believe that your story (or interpretation) is more real than Truth. All stories lead away from peace and eventually to suffering. So, you can go through your stories and leave them behind by questioning their validity.

Can you experience something without creating a story about it or the people involved? This is not easy, but Grace is ready to take you beyond the reaches of the story-creating mind, and into your unconditioned heart.

Ultimately, what form your affection and actions take will be determined by whether you dwell in your stories about the human facts, or with transcendent Truth.

Anything that enters your experience will at some point leave. Where we get stuck in life is when we try to grasp onto something because we want it to stay, or want it to leave. We can be attached to trying to hold it close, or push it away.

When you are willing to free everything that can be released, you are left with what you are. And what you are, has been, is, and ever will be enough. You are the way infinite Life shows up.

A perception of insufficiency is inaccurate. Always. Scarcity or lack is not a condition that exists in the changeless Universe. Whenever it appears to your awareness, it is simply an invitation. Scarcity = an invitation, to believe in a mirage.

Here are some common invitations to believe in mirages:
- A body in lack
- A self-concept in lack
- A neighbor in lack
- A relationship in lack
- An organization in lack
- A nation in lack
- A bank account in lack
- An environment in lack
- A church in lack

What mirages do is appear to your perception, and ask you to believe in them. If you are immobilized in fear, they will stay in your view. If you are willing to see through them, then as you approach them, when you get close enough, they disappear.

You cannot be subject to a mirage, because they have no power to do anything. You are dealing with and experiencing your perception, not a separate power, substance, or condition.

The mirage of scarcity does not become abundance. When your belief in the hallucination of limitation is unlearned, it disappears, and you then experience that which was always there. When your perception of the mirage vanishes, you see what was pre-existing and changeless.

A tragedy can appear to shake the very foundation upon which we exist day-to-day. This is completely understandable. It often makes us question everything we hold as real and true.

There is no one "right" way to look at a tragedy in your life. But, there are ways to grow through the experience, when you are ready. We can't force this growth... When you are ready may be when you find seeds strewn from the devastating experience beginning to gently give birth to a wider and deeper affection than you had even before the event.

At some point your resilient identity starts to re-emerge in a new form. You may have felt buried and out of it, like a bulb in the winter, but now find yourself meekly poking through the rugged soil of daily experience, to breathe new air. Imagine what a bulb might be feeling as it sprouts new shoots and starts to feel unmistakably larger, pulled toward the light.

This is not something we fabricate with the mind, to make things somehow "better." It is not something we "do." It is something that grows within our heart ... until it can no longer be contained, and but must be released. We can't stop it. It is the activity and presence of Grace.

What can you do to help this natural growth process? Be open to it. When you are ready. You will know. And until then, it's OK. You are just how you need to be. Always.

We can never really know why a senseless act occurs. And apparently, we don't need to. But, we can feel what it calls forth in us.

What it calls forth depends upon what you have been prioritizing in life, prior to the event. For you:
- It could call forth anger, rage, despair and/or hopelessness
- It could call forth blame of an individual and/or group
- It could be a wake-up call: a realization that you have taken much for granted
- It could be a call to really learn how to forgive what feels unforgivable
- It could be a call to action to pray in a deeper, more humble way than you ever have
- It could be a call to walk into the dark side of your self that you may have been holding hostage through avoidance, and face transcendence
- It could be a call to offer amends with a family member or friend you have been holding in abeyance (and be OK with any response received)
- It could be a call to reach out to those who may be feeling unloved in this moment
- It could be a call to stop thinking you have everything (or anything) figured out, and finally let Grace prioritize your life
- It could be a call to see and feel the immaculate, indestructible oneness of Life

I'm sure you are noticing what it is calling forth in you. Whatever it is, please be conscious of it, accept it, learn from it, and walk clearer in your learning.

We need your heart's clarity.

If we are missing someone who we think is gone, what we are missing is a misperception. Misperceptions bring pain because they separate existence into beliefs of hypothetical isolation. This is an illusion based in a delusion.

Coexistence with the Divine, and therefore all being, is the only fabric of Life. No one can leave that substance, any more than a number can leave math. Where can they go?

Coexistence is the only constant. All is present, and this can be experienced through humbly opening our yearning hearts to feeling the presence of Love without egoing (pre-determining the form it should take). We can open to be the space where Grace lands.

Authentic Self-realization

You can't screw up your life.
It is not possible.

When it feels like you did,
your constant companions are
guilt, shame, regret, disappointment,
confusion, and resentment.
These are based on
a misperception of reality.
Nothing you have ever done
has you permanently stuck.

You will experience
this awakening freedom
as you open to every moment
being an adventure
in which you embrace:

Listening
to Grace to go beyond the mind's ruts
(which opens you to)

Unlearning
limiting stories and beliefs
(which opens you to)

Discovery
of new understanding
(which opens you to)

Witnessing
with gratitude the benefits and blessings all around
(which opens you to)

Celebrating
that Love was, is, and ever will be
governing us all without a flaw.

To practice total acceptance, is extremely difficult for the
mind. This is especially true in situations like the rash of
recent mass shootings. The mind feels its primary role is to be
the detective and judge for right and wrong. This is not what
is needed right now. It is a decoy.

The effect of forgoing judgment is that your windshield stays
clean, and you are given the unprejudiced clarity to see what
is in front of you, with unbiased eyes and a broad heart. This
then frees you to be driven completely by Grace, without distractions, in your authentic response to each moment.

This is what is most needed. Now and always.

When do you feel the deepest peace? What is that for you?

Whether it is when you are doing something, or being something, this could be the time to do it, and to be it.

Your witness of peace may unexpectedly rainbow through the dark clouds, and help another regain the promise of what appears to be lost.

We are made to be beams of Light: the flow of Love's radiation. The impact we have is not up to us. It comes from Grace, is carried through Grace, and arrives by Grace.

To grasp is human, to release is divine.

D o you have any of these long-term needs?

- I need to get married (and have a family).
- I need to get divorced.
- I need to make $_____.
- I need to be enlightened.
- I need to get the perfect job.
- I need to get published.
- I need to get healed.
- I need to learn to heal instantaneously.
- I need to _____ ...

Each of these are conditional delusions about your future happiness that you may have locked yourself into. If so, you are now chained to their walls, suffering because you think you are in lack. Nothing could be farther from the truth.

You lack nothing. You've got the goods. We all do. It is how we are made and maintained.

Any of these may occur in your experience, but to think you will be happier when they occur is making you miss the Kingdom of Heaven. Heaven is now, within your consciousness. It is the current event.

Surrender your caterpillar demands to Grace, and watch your affections chrysalis into a beauty and freedom beyond any plan you could ever concoct.

One Infinite Being

All One
Beyond you and God
Beyond "and"
Beyond delineation, circumference, center, parts
Beyond mine, yours, theirs, self-concepts, misperceptions
Beyond good vs. evil, right vs. wrong, judgments
Just One

All Now
Beyond time, development, maturity, aging
Beyond starts, stops, history, soon to be, linear logic
Just pure 360-degree awareness of Vitality

All Here
Beyond location, boundaries, more, less
Just, that from which everything springs
That in which everything resides
That to which everything points
That which everything is

All Open
Beyond grasp, cling, gather, keep, memorize, hoard
Beyond need, control, figure out, hover, smother
Beyond preoccupation, fixation, obsession, addiction
Just, that which is always freely available

Sense our magnificent Presence
Feel into this
Our one infinite Being

If there is one infinite Consciousness that is the source, substance, and life of all being, how could it possibly make a part of its creation unsafe?

All reality is connected in and as this inseparable, eternal Oneness. This is pure safety. Who you are in Truth is forever here and now, and can't be at risk.

So, the images, and corresponding feelings that imply that one is unsafe, can't be accurate or true. They are based on believing concepts that suggest an alternative, hypothetical, limited identity.

When you realize that these thoughts are misidentifications of the one Self, it is the path to peace for every relationship on the planet.

Any step to peace that bypasses transforming your individual consciousness from duality to oneness, is egoic, temporary, and doomed to fail.

When something does not go the way we think it should, it is interesting to notice our reactions.

Two weeks ago my email program sent me a note saying that my database had some errors and it needed to be rebuilt. For seven hours it tried to rebuild itself and then it said that some files are corrupt. At this point I could not receive or send emails, so I called Microsoft for help. After working with the rep for two hours, she said, "Your files are permanently lost: irretrievable."

Two feelings arose simultaneously: "No way! This can't be happening!" And, "This is happening, and there are some unknown blessings here that are yet to be revealed. This will be such fun to see what they are, and how this situation leaves me in a better place."

What was particularly fascinating about this was that I didn't do anything to create either feeling. The desperation thought appeared and it was like Grace caught it and said, "Sorry desperation, I have been here forever and have this covered."

I'm learning and experiencing that this is always the case, in every possible situation.

Just because something or someone enters or leaves your experience, it does not in any way increase or diminish your value or worth. You may experience:

- A compliment or criticism
- A promotion or pink slip
- Abundance or debt
- A hug or slap
- A marriage or divorce
- A birth or death
- Morality or immorality
- A one-putt or four-putt
- An "A" or "F"
- A championship or defeat
- Health or sickness
- Remembering or forgetting
- An ascension, resurrection, or crucifixion

Before, during, and after any of these, you are still you:

- Spotless
- Incomparable
- Immaculate
- Irreplaceable
- Whole
- Innocent
- Complete
- Unbroken
- Beautiful
- Authentic
- Pure
- One with Life
- Beyond any of these words or concepts, and that to which they each point

Man is not something that comes and goes. The only things that come and go are our delusions about man.

Death is when to our perception, someone no longer exists in the form we were used to. To the friends of fellow caterpillars, it would likely look like that when a caterpillar enters the chrysalis, it dies. We know this is not the case.

When the caterpillar friends only use the senses that were activated at the beginning of the caterpillar stage, they believe the passage on this planet is all there is to life. This is logical.

But, when these friends have learned to access senses that transcend this stage, they maintain an awareness that is anchored in actual reality. Every caterpillar that goes into the chrysalis and then right on through to the butterfly, knows with total clarity, that life is perpetual.

When a friend changes form before us, we can celebrate what they now know for sure: Life is the only constant. Their identity is untouched by transition and transformation.

Over the last few months I have been watching with a dear friend as he transitioned through and beyond this phase of life. Here are some of the lessons we are learning.

A defining condition of duality is the belief in opposites. We noticed the mind trying to control either how the positive side of life should show up more, or the negative side should show up less. It tried in vain to hold the right beliefs or doctrines to get the physical results it wanted. It tried to maintain a pre-determined certainty of what "health" looks like.

We saw that while we all are accustomed to these activities, it was a useless war that no one will ever win, given that the mind empowered it with the convicted premise of two opposing sides.

When we embraced an unconditioned consciousness of pure Oneness, the dualistic boundaries became translucent as a new dimension of Light was experienced. Life was felt as an ever-freeing adventure into the Unknown, filled with endless surprises and transformative discoveries.

We saw that whatever came our way, instead of being met with judgment, was welcomed with gratitude. The premise here was that no matter what experience we go through, we are safe because Heaven has no opposite. This extinguishes the shadow of death, because nothing exists but the Light of Life: the presence of Love.

When we remove the belief in an opposite, we are left with One. And this One, which includes us, is Now.

I am confident that we are each clearer on this than ever before. Thank you precious brother, for laying down your life for this friend.

Y ou are the way Life is forever happening. At this point, you may believe the delusion that you are the way a separate mortal began, is living, and will end.

Because you are the former, everything you appear to go through as a mortal can be transcended in each moment, and the matchless presence of Reality experienced. As this occurs, the belief that you will perish erodes.

Notice this moment as it arrives, lives, and dies. This is the only death you will ever experience, the passing of now. But you are not sad when a moment passes because the next moment is already present, and then it instantly passes, giving place to the next, and so on, forever. You don't ever fear that it won't be now.

So, you will never die because you are the way Life as Consciousness is forever happening. You are not was.

Chapter 11

You Are Now

This moment is unfolding as it is, not because of what you have done. Your experience is not the accumulation of what you have done. You are not your source. (Sorry ego.)

Your life is the way Life is showing up in your awareness. You experience it as heaven or hell by taking the full Light of Being and letting it come through as unfiltered grace, or by passing it through the strainer of your ego's attempt to direct or control your experience.

When you drop the control strainer you experience your authentic Self, and lose all concern for a future. This moment is so delicious, you can't even think about the next bite!

As long as you are waiting for a specific, pre-determined kind of good to occur, you are missing the fullness of the good that is occurring. Will the present good ever be enough for you?

Why not try it this moment and see?

You are now

Are you working toward
demonstrating eternal life?
It's too late.
This is it.
How could it be any other?
You are living the now of eternal Life.
It will never not be now.

So, whatever it is
you are worried about
will not last.
Or, put another way:
you will outlast
whatever it is
you are worried about.

The only thing eternal
is your Life.
Everything else
is in the process
of disappearing.

If you are anxious about the future, it is because you are referencing the past and projecting it into a hypothetical reality. You may have had so many similar experiences in the past, that it is very challenging to not expect that the future will be the same. This is where we can get stuck.

This moment never happened before. It is 100% original: pure Divine innovation. Can you celebrate that, versus being concerned that it may not be the way you think it should be? Can you embrace that your role is not to predict or control the future? Your role is not to know what is next.

What if you let your thoughts of the future be informed by Grace? Will Grace deliver the same old, same old? Impossible. You can completely miss the revolutionary brilliance of now, by viewing it through a lens clouded with expectancy.

Please remember, this is Love's show, not yours. Love is the Director and you are the directed.

As long as you believe there is even one person outside the Kingdom of Heaven, you are not awake to the present reality of Grace here and now.

There are no possible exclusions in One Infinite Being.

Your most precious resource is where you allow your attention to rest. It determines the quality of your entire life experience. Are willing to live and work at the calling and pace of Grace?

This is Heaven

If you don't believe it, it doesn't matter.
It is still heaven.
It will just feel like hell.

I invite you to answer the questions below for yourself, and see where they lead you.

- What have you outgrown that you are not willing to leave?

- What perceived benefits do you receive from holding on to what you have outgrown?

- How does clutching to what you have outgrown, reinforce your self-esteem (high or low)?

Here's some examples of a responses:
- What have you outgrown that you are not willing to leave? The desire to do what pleases others.

- What perceived benefits do you receive from holding on to what you have outgrown? I get to feel good because other people like me when I please them.

- How does clutching to what you have outgrown, reinforce your self-esteem? It makes me believe I am a good guy because others like me. (Can you see how easy it would be to get stuck here?)

You will never experience the future.

You may make plans for an ideal future, but you cannot plan how each moment will unfold. Everything happens for the first time, in each moment, and you cannot determine one of them. Realizing this can feel scary because you are so used to believing you are controlling your life.

You are the manifestation of this one infinite Moment that we call Life. You are not doing something to make this Moment happen. You are the way this Moment is unfolding.

At this point, you get to wake up, and yield to the one divine Moment, or fall asleep and dream you are controlling your life. But, can you really control a dream? Not at all. So, thinking you can is just further proof that you are dreaming. In your dream, you have an image of yourself that you are controlling how your life goes.

So what is your role? Awaken to this Moment as it is happening. Celebrate that you don't know (or need to know) what will happen next. And be open to watching each jigsaw piece fit perfectly in the marvelous puzzle, governed by Grace.

Listen Fresh

This moment never happened before.
You are new
now,
and now,
and now.

We weren't made for ruts of atrophy.
And Now.

Who's view of reality are you living in?
Nature is unfolding you.
And Now.

Your purpose is always ripe.
We don't have to wait to give,
or to release the outgrown.
And Now.

Away from now
is then,
or when.

Then is stale,
and when
is too green to pick.

Listen fresh.
Harvest Now.

And Now.

Many of us desire more patience when something is not happening when, or how, we think it should. We have a plan and reality is not cooperating. So what do we do? We wait, we get frustrated and bored, we get concerned, we distract ourselves, we count things, we judge others…and the list goes on.

What if you used those moments, right then and there, to take a deep breath, and be fully present with exactly what is happening in front of you?

Each amazing moment is occurring only once. Open up wherever you are: listen, watch. See with new eyes. Don't miss it. This IS Life. Can you feel it? Don't miss it. Grace doesn't do the future. We are only now.

L ife is so much simpler than we make it. It is lived in the present moment. That is the only option.

You get to either live from that naturally awake, enlightened, and free standpoint, or miss it completely as you project your memories into the present, and then the future.

These projections can become the fabric of your relationships and your whole approach to career and life. They keep you stuck in dramatic cycles of lack, limitation, anxiety, sadness, and resentment. These stories, based on your memories, can feel so present that you actually believe them and identify with them. They can form your concept of yourself.

Enter Unlearning: realizing that although the stories feel like they are you, they are not. In the same way, a stamp stuck on an envelope cannot become the envelope, nor can it change the envelope's innate purity and wholeness.

Come back to now, without your past or future pining. In this stillness you will find the part of you that is always at peace, as you are fed by Grace.

Life is one forever, amazing moment, inviting us into YES! Our conditioned mind misses the invitation and thus keeps going to watch the same movie over and over and over.

Often we will project ourselves into the movie so much that we get attached to the outcome of specific scenes: especially the ones called "If only . . ." All the while, Life offers all of itself to us, as our very being, each moment.

You can't possibly know what will happen in the next moment. To have an expectation about what it is supposed to be like is suicide for your happiness and peace, and a complete waste of time.

If what does happen is what you expected, that's really a shame, because it will likely encourage you to develop more expectations about what should happen. And then you may actually try to live your life so that you can control what happens to you, and how others treat you, and even use spirituality to bring this about.

An alternative? Let Life reveal itself, and love (and learn from) whatever shows up.

You can't control this moment. You can only be it.

No matter what is going on, can you find the good in this moment and celebrate it? Is not this what God is doing, seeing Her creation? If this is what your Source is doing then this is also your natural state. See if you can do this for an entire minute.

The moment you move away from now and focus on how something should be different, your mind enters a dream of confusion. This produces fear, anger, envy, sadness, suffering: wasted moments miss-interpreting Life.

Celebrate the endless moments of good, right now. With this heart-seeing, you will lose the self that is focused on a regretful past or an anxious future, and experience the abundance of this perfect moment. Welcome to Reality!

You Are Right Now Enough

When you are in your "zone,"
all your needs are already met.

Why?
Because you have
no consciousness of self
in those moments,
so you need nothing
to complete you.

There is no waiting,
no anxious wondering,
no future,
and no past regrets.
You are fully engaged,
100% being
in whatever you are doing.
This is Life revealing you.
This is Reality.

So is it possible
to always live in your zone?
Yes.
It is your pure, natural, free,
transcendent nature.

This false "figure out my life" self
evaporates
as your authentic Now-Self
displaces it.

So if you have an important decision to make,
let your love radiate forth
in this (and each) moment,
and you may find
you act your way into an answer.

Believe it or not,
right now is enough.
And, you are always and only,
now.

Openness to this one ever-unfolding-Moment is what
a flower naturally does in being itself. This one perfect
Moment is Life itself, and reveals every detail of our experience. Nothing is left out.

If you are not trusting that, you might just be trying to control your way into heaven. Might be worth an honest look.

Ever notice how hard it is to celebrate the ineffable joy of each moment when you are concerned about something that isn't going as you think it should? Think of how much you are missing when your thoughts are boomeranging back to your story about how your world should be a certain way.

The most magnificent beauty is unfolding right before your eyes, and it is as if you are in another world, encased in your limited frame of reference. Your focus is so tightly wrapped around your perspective, that it is strangling your clarity and peace.

Take a breath: a really deep one. Seriously. See if you can release your grip on trying to control how Life is unfolding. Would everything fall completely apart if you weren't the one needing to hold it all together?

See what happens when you rely on an Intelligence that includes you, versus one that comes from you.

The Divine is here

Simple, natural, beautiful order.
Ordered, simple, natural beauty.
Natural, beautiful, ordered simplicity.
Beautiful, ordered, simple nature.
Such is Life.
Such are We.

Do you ever find yourself living for the next thing you
have to look forward to? Have you ever felt depressed
because you have nothing to look forward to?

The ego is conditioned to attract thought away from the actu-
ality of the present, to the dream of the future. The only way
to fulfillment and deep peace is to enter through whatever
experience you are having here and now. If it is challenging,
instead of fleeing it, experience it fully. It is here to be used
and learned from, not dreamed away from. The sole portal to
the Divine is this moment.

The pure flowing expression of Love is all that is ultimately going on. This is Reality. The human experience is one of flashing thought pictures, which are forever coming and going.

If the flashing thought pictures are believed and interpreted as real and true, then the mind is not empty or clear. It is sidetracked, distracted and confused: living in a fantasy world of its own stories. What is experienced is chaos. This attentive attachment to flickering illusions blocks the experience of pure Love in us, and is what we experience as suffering.

When pictures flow through an empty or clear mind, they are not believed. They are noticed. What is experienced is the uninterrupted perfection and order of Reality. Here we find ourselves in a state of constant gratitude, celebration, and awe, independent of the pictures.

You don't need anyone, or anything, to change for you to be happy. These mindsets have fixed happiness into the future.

If those people or things do change, you may find you have a short span of happiness, until very quickly the mind does it again, and gets you to think something else needs to be different to make you really happy. This is the game the mind is programmed to play. It is called happier, better, more…all based in the future. The problem is not that the mind does this, it is that you are believing it.

Next time this comes up, see if you can find the part of you that is already happy, at peace, and grateful. It is always there because this is the very fiber of your being. This is what you are.

The mind gets you to look outside, and to the future, for what already exists within you, now. Crazy, I know. This is why we need to unlearn the whole way our mind operates.

You

No matter what has happened to you,
no matter what is happening to you,
no matter what will happen to you,
there is Something
always happening as you,
that maintains you.

This is your Constant.
You are maintained.
This began before your conscious memory.
It continues when you forget.
You do not sustain yourself.
You are being lived:
All of you
By all of It
In a forever of nows

For one week I was in the presence of a woman who is spiritually awake.

The ego provides no distractions for her. All I felt from her every moment was pure, unconditional, holy love. I felt seen, like never before. Her view and experience of reality provided the tangible presence of Grace.

She has no past about which she feels guilt or resentment. She has no future about which she is concerned or anxious. She has no fear.

Her example revealed to me how often I unconsciously use my past deficient beliefs as a reference, and then project them into my experience, creating a future I fear.

She is so completely and naturally focused on living in the present as the only access point to Truth, that it was sometimes hard for my rational mind to follow her logic. I felt intuitive clarity, and like I had to be OK without my usual reasoning. She walked me into the unknown, and left me there to resonate and ripen with Grace.

We are each on a path that has no destination. If that is discouraging, then you may want to sit quietly with that thought and see if it resonates at all. If it does not resonate, you don't need to read the next paragraph. Just keep striving to reach all your goals.

If the point is not to get somewhere, why are you in such a hurry to arrive? Maybe the point is to wake up from the full time job of dreaming about an ideal future. Maybe you are to literally treasure each moment as you are acting from the only place you will ever be. Here.

Chapter 12

Deep Yearning

Within you there is a deep yearning, that is calling you to authentically want to be who you are. It was put there before you arrived here, and is fountaining you forth.

Most of us have not unlearned enough to recognize, listen to, and feel into, our deepest calling. We are not trained to surrender to, and receive, our heart's song.

It is never too late to open this room in your home. Give yourself completely to it, as if you were falling into a comfy chair. Let everything else go. This is how Life is meant to be lived.

This Has Happened
or Will Happen to You

Subsisting upon the surface tension of life
you were solidly believing
you were (pick one or more) separate, lost, abandoned,
worthless, unforgivable, beyond hope, empty,
unlovable,
alone,
divided, two...
until Grace surrounded you
from the inside out,
and for an eternal moment
the two was severed into One,
and the never-ending echoes of condemnation vanished
and you were so expanded in that moment
that thinking stopped and being appeared
and you heard The Song,
and now the harmonics has you, even when you forget,
and you know beyond knowing
that there is a transcendent Presence
that is all of you and more than you.

This was the beginning of your rebirth,
and nothing has been the same since.

And if this hasn't happened yet,
just dance to the sweetest rhythm you hear in the womb

There is something within each of us that deeply yearns to be on fire in our oneness with the Divine. Throw everything you've got into this fire! Don't hold back. This is a fire that purifies not consumes. It refines you into who and what you are. It burns stories based on memories, and melts anxiety. It reveals authenticity.

Most of us are covered in conscious and unconscious underbrush, thinking we know so much. Come on! Burn that too. Start over with an empty mind, and a new heart, right now. You belong to Love.

Can you define what you really want in life in a way that no person or circumstance can ever interfere with you receiving it?

If so, you are free.

You don't need to learn how to hear sounds. It flows within your natural capabilities. You have the goods. You hear sounds all day long…effortlessly. You just naturally allow your attention to rest where you choose.

In the same way you don't need to learn how to hear your Inner Teacher, or the voice of Grace. This is your natural, intuitive, spiritual inclination. It is as natural as breathing.

You have the goods. You just allow your attention to rest where the deepest yearning in your heart leads it. There, you will always find the presence of Grace guiding you.

What if we could see and feel that God shows up in each of us as our deepest yearning? And what if this yearning was the substance and essence of our being?

Then, because there is one God, it would follow that we all share the same yearning, the same being. And there could be no exceptions to this. Ever.

One infinite God, showing up as one infinite yearning, in one infinite being. Separation in this scenario is simply inaccurate.

And what if this is true, regardless of our beliefs?

Just One.

What do you really want in life? What is your deepest yearning? Are you willing to commit your life to continually answering these questions?

Here's an example: My deepest yearning is to love without judgment, and to unlearn when I can't. This is the reason I do what I do. Anything.

In doing this I find some people and situations I can love without judgment, and some I cannot. When I can, I naturally love selflessly. When I cannot, I get excited because this means I get to unlearn what is blocking my ability to love.

So far, the only thing that has blocked my expression of love is a concept of myself or others as deficient in some way. Each time these self-concepts are dissolved, the natural expression of love returns.

So, I'm either expressing unconditional love, or learning to love without judgment. Both fulfill my deepest yearning. This may sound very simple. And, it is.

Until you have surrendered your deepest yearnings to Grace, and found the presence of Love in your heart, you will never find the love you are seeking. You will feel as if you have a bottomless void that you are waiting for others to fill.

In your deepest knowing, you get that nothing outside can ever fill you up on the inside. You get that new paint on your house will not make for a warmer sense of home. They are not even related.

You know when you have found the Kingdom of Heaven within your heart, because your deepest yearning is transformed from wanting something to simply being. The universal oneness of the love you feel naturally embraces and includes yourself and others! It transcends the personal.

There is an absolute conviction within each of us that all is irrevocably well. We just find it at different times.

Once this arrives, nothing will ever get your attention the way it used to.

"**I** am playing it safe in my life in terms of spiritual awakening."

"I am too busy to create room for game-changing spiritual breakthroughs."

"I am feeling like I am maintaining the status quo, and given all I have on my plate, that is good enough."

"I am so focused on serving others that I don't create deep and meaningful spaces to see who I am through new eyes and a new heart?"

These are statements I hear echoed from people all the time. If one of these fits your pattern, I invite you (and urge you) to listen deeply, humbly, and authentically for your response to this question: What matters most in your life?

The Search

I walk in the sand alone, ... thinking of love.
Once again   I'll see if I can figure it out.

I ponder if peace of heart is   an illusion.
When I think I've grasped it,   I'm afraid I'll lose it.
Will I ever get it right?   Is it too late?
I am growing   impatient.

Nothing is near except   my hollow shell
that doesn't fulfill.
All my analyzing   is repelling others' affections.
My crowded beach   is actually empty.
I am stranded,   stuck in the quicksand
                        of well-intentioned self-absorption.
                                                Again.
This scene is a rerun I'm sick of staring at.

While my mind keeps searching the shore for clues, ...
my arid heart   remembers Love.

Having reached the mud flats,
I lean toward   Your forever incoming tide.
Finding my inlet ready,   You enter.

My wet eyes still strain to understand why.
"Let go of the shore,   I've got you..."
You whisper through my feelings.
I feel You rise in me as   I give up the struggle to get.

Your gentle current   lifts and turns me from me to You.
I am gradually carried to   where all is one.
Suspended in Your embrace   I am given to,
                                           completely.

As You channel me back toward land,   my eyes
are buoyed up to   see
something besides myself.   So many precious people!

As I ride Your crest to   the shore,
You place me   on solid ground.

Feeling   purposefully sustained by You,
I now walk the beach freely,   without needing tomorrow,
                                      committed to being,
                                           like You.

The conditioned mind is practically invisible to us because we use it almost exclusively all our waking hours. It creates judgments and stories based on accepted and unquestioned beliefs. It can drive our lives and keep us caught in cycles of non-progressive behavior.

This is why it is worthwhile to continually disrupt and unlearn your conditioned mind so you can awaken to your unconditioned, Grace-impelled consciousness.

Have there been times in your life when you have consciously broken your routines and received deep moments of clarity? What were some of these? How often do you do this?

Here are some "disruptions" that have transformed my view of reality and myself over the past few decades:

- Spending days in silence
- Taking days alone in nature to listen and observe
- Fasting
- Deeply and quietly questioning stressful situations
- Running at and embracing the darkness (the parts of my experience that are the scariest, and where I usually avoid going)
- Doing activities outside my comfort zone (e.g. skydiving, distance running, vision quests)
- Taking daily dictations from Grace
- Dedicating 20% of my day to spiritual practices
- Annually attending a variety of programs that challenge my view of spirituality and humanity
- Experiencing cultures dramatically different from my own (e.g. in West Africa, Israel, Palestine)
- Reading broadly and contemplatively

Life is too precious to live it in ruts (even comfortable ones)! Let's burst through our boundaries and explore the Unknown!

Are you willing to be transformed into the divine model and order, or are you trying to get the divine to conform to your pre-determined model and order? Every day your life consciously or unconsciously answers this question.

When the mind is perplexed and can't find the answers it thinks it wants and even needs, Grace keeps resonating in our yearning hearts. It may come more as a silent, sweet embrace, a deep feeling that echoes, "I have it. I have you. The timing, and yes all, is Mine."

Learning to fall into that embrace, rather than the ceaseless analyzing in the vacuum of a mind not ready to yield, this is my prayer.

What do you do to distract yourself from what really matters?

Are you OK with this? If you were training for a crucial life-goal, like making the Olympic team, would allowing this distraction be an option for you? Can you face this honestly?

What if you said "No" to this diversion, and asked Grace what, if anything, to replace it with? Perhaps, that for which you most deeply yearn for in your life would be more present.

Are you in?

How do you kindle the fire in your heart? Are you humbly fanning it each day so that the glow is not blown out by society, doctrines, or your continual reference to your past?

Your deepest yearning is the presence of God, flowing in you and as you. As you surrender your decisions to this pulsating Sea of Compassion, it will reveal a clarity that is beyond the intellect: the unerring compass of wisdom.

Temptation is just an invitation to fulfill "a desire" at a level that will not get you what you really want. There is nothing wrong with you for having this craving.

As you listen for, and feel into, your deepest yearning, beneath today's longing, just sit with what comes up, in stillness. You don't need to do anything else. Just be conscious that this innate yearning is alive in you. It is there to awaken you to the experience of Oneness.

Grace meets your yearning, and brings you home to Love.

When you are in touch with what you really want in life, and totally going for it, it puts everything else in perspective. You rarely lose sight of the bigger picture because your deepest yearning drives everything. You feel Grace ordering your day.

You don't do boredom (who has time for that?!).

You exercise a disciplined structure when it is called for. You completely let go of structure when that is called for.

You don't have fixed expectations about the future, but rather, embrace that you don't know what will happen next, and don't need to.

You don't lie to yourself about how you are showing up. You face yourself without judgment, and celebrate that there may be something to unlearn.

Even after a discouraging day where you wonder… "Why am I even pursuing this activity?" the next morning your Grace-driven yearning re-emerges, and you can't wait to get back at it. It is experienced as resilience.

These are some of the reasons why it is so vital to be in touch with what you really want in life. Without it, you may find yourself drifting into procrastination, frustration, self-doubt, and self-condemnation.

Tonight's Dialogue

Me: "One?"

God: "Yes, just One."

Me: "But, I thought it was You, and me and everyone and everything."

God: "Just One."

Me: "I don't get it."

God: "Good. Now stay there. Don't try to get it. Be excited that you don't get it. You ready?"

Me: "Yes. I am convinced that I don't know where this is going."

God: "Good. You don't really ever know where anything is going. That's My job."

Me: "Good point. Thanks."

God: "So here we go. Back to One: You are not Me, but I AM all of you."

Me: "Wow... That feels so...humbling...like...I'm not steering my own ship...Any of it...That's new..."

God: "I govern all of you because I AM all of you. One. Just marinate in it."

The most frequent question I receive is: "What can I do to sustain a feeling of deep peace?"

Are you are in an endless pursuit of trying to add things and ideas to yourself so you can feel whole and complete? Most of us are.

An alternative approach is to release the nonstop seeking, and experience the Self that is already at peace. How do you find that Self? Stop seeking. Just stop. See what arises in consciousness when you are not wishing for something different.

The thought may come up, "If I'm not trying to find something better, then I'll always be stuck with this empty feeling." Is that really true? How would you know, if all you are doing is grasping (and gasping) for the next fix?

Just stop. Take a deep breath, and give Grace a chance to emerge. Have the conscious experience of not seeking, and see what happens.

In the previous insight I invited you to take a break from your addiction to seeking, and see what happens. Our conditioning makes it almost impossible not to seek. Did you try it? Could you stop seeking for even five minutes? What was it like? (If you didn't try it yet, you could try it now.)

When you see yourself as a seeker, the ego gets you to believe that you are seeking something you lack, and therefore are innately deficient. It is your belief in a deficient self-image that keeps you locked in the cycle of scarcity, atrophy, and inconsistent peace.

Here's another way to view this: When you do not feel the presence of Grace, you yearn deeply for it. This deep yearning is not the ego. It is actually your divine nature pulsing in you. It is calling you back to your Self, to the Oneness of all Being. It is your authentic nature yearning to be expressed. It is in there! It is you!

When you no longer see yourself as a separate, deficient seeker, but realize your sacred yearning is coming from the Kingdom of Heaven WITHIN you, you may feel yourself opening to a field of Grace. Try it. Have a quiet walk in that field. Open your heart, and see what emerges.

In the past two insights you were invited to relax your seeking muscle, and feel the deep divine yearning within you that is the proof that you've got the goods!

Did you notice that there is not a lot you are doing in this approach? What we are unlearning is that it's not what YOU do that counts; it's what Grace does! If you think you have to do it all, you will unconsciously by-pass Grace and try to replicate these fireflying feelings of peace. (You will also exhaust yourself.)

You are the actual dance of Grace. Right now. As you surrender to the sacred yearning within you, you may begin to notice that your experience is ordered for you. There will be a softening to your demeanor as the tendency to judge yourself or others fades. It's no longer up to you to run your world.

You will find yourself listening to Grace if a decision is needed. You will consciously experience the way Life is living you, and everyone.

One of the by-products? Real Grace-sustained peace.

What really matters to you?

Can you identify what you need to say "No" to in your life, so that what really matters can have space to thrive?

When you want some thing (a person, food, thing, acceptance, love, etc.) to satisfy a longing you have, what you really yearn for is the conscious experience of what you already are. You need nothing outside of you to fulfill you.

When you are fully expressing yourself in your zone, you are so used up (so to speak), that there is simply nothing left in you that needs attention.

Are you yearning to experience the Divine in such a way that you feel guided day-by-day, even moment-by-moment? Most of us desire this, but many do not experience it. Why? Here's one possible reason.

The conditioned mind is so engrained in ruts (even spiritual ruts) that it has a hard time seeing past its time-honored walls. When you feel imprisoned in a cycle of uninspired sameness, check your assumptions. There may be religious rhetoric or doctrines that you have accepted as the only way to reach the Divine.

What if you met someone who was living everything you are hoping for within your spiritual assumptions, but they were coming at it from an entirely different perspective? Would you be genuinely interested in learning from their approach?

Have you limited the channels through which Grace can reach man? Grace will reach anyone, but it may require humiliation of the ego, and a willingness to be authentically and vulnerably open to abandoning your sacred stuckness.

Chapter 13

•

Showing Up
Open

There are no special conditions needed for you to be reached by Grace.

Sometimes we think the Divine will not be present because we fall short in what we feel we need to do in order to receive it. Rubbish.

What if we just opened our hearts to the awareness of spontaneous Grace now, and dropped any future expectations about the when, where and how?

I like to experience life as non-stop opportunities to commune with Grace.

We tend to look at life through a hair-width sliver and think this is all there is. This drastically limits our view of the galaxy of abundance that is waiting to reveal itself within our uncorked consciousness.

If you are feeling a pressure that your life is not going as it is supposed to, you might ask yourself, "Says who?" Who is the authority that you believe is judging you? Is it a person, a doctrine, your self, God? None of that matters.

Your life is unfolding exactly as it needs to for you to learn what you are ready to. Embrace the lessons of discovering that you are not how your experience is unfolding, you are the one watching it come and go.

The entire universe is designed to point you to Oneness. When you feel deeply peaceful, you are awake and experiencing this Presence.

Whenever you don't feel peaceful, you have fallen asleep. If someone close to you treats you in a way that bothers you, you may get angry, or afraid, because the person is disturbing your dream. You think, "What's going on? They're supposed to love me."

This is exactly what they are doing! They are there to wake up the part of you that is asleep, dreaming the dream of separation. (They may not know this, but that is irrelevant.) Anything that disturbs your peace is a warning light that your thought is not aligned with Reality. What a gift! Are you ready to receive it?

Just show up!

Shoes on ready to dance.
Ears on ready to listen.
Heart on ready to forgive.
Head off!

There can be a subtle mirage that arises when you draw conclusions on spiritual matters. The ego can use this to encourage you to feel like you have something important figured out. From this state, the mind closes down around itself because it believes it has grasped the way things are. Think of this as a spiritualized ego.

Here's how it can play out: When you have a need, you may find you just go to what you know, vs. dropping all concerns into the Unknown, and listening to Grace. If you are not alert, you may find you have developed dependence upon your tried and true prayers and concepts, vs. dependence on God.

What would it feel and look like for you to have more practical moment-by-moment reliance on the Unknown than the known? Let's hit the streets with our answers, together.

It is not Cause and effect, as in two separate events. It would be better represented as Causeffect. It is not Sun and light, but Sunlight. Where does the sun stop and light begin? There is no delay in manifestation or expression. Everything is happening all at once, now. And, now never ends.

Humanly we don't always experience this oneness of Being, but that does not mean it is not the way it works. It just means that our individual and collective conditioning is ignorant of this aspect of reality.

What's cool is that we get to unlearn or release our attachment to our imaginations and beliefs that suggest that Oneness is not the norm. See if you can notice when you are believing in severance, division, disconnection or twoness. It is embedded in the very fabric of egoic consciousness. It is the source of all struggles, battles, and greed for control.

Bottom line is that you don't need to wait to witness Oneness. It's not arriving eventually. Its all there is. In the same breath, demanding that you experience it now won't work either (that's control).

Just disengage from your will, know that Oneness is the real deal, open your heart to loving your connection to everyone, and let Grace land. You will feel the presence of authentic Oneness.

The broader our frame of reference, the more we don't know. For example, you may know where you are sitting right now, but you really have no idea where you are in the scope of the physical universe! You are a speck, on a dot, that rotates and revolves around a small star dot, in a small galaxy, one of countless other galaxies. And everything is moving!

So, if your physical frame of reference is infinite, you will never know exactly where you are. Can you embrace not knowing this?

Now, if the spiritual universe is also infinite, and that is your frame of reference, than similarly, you will never know exactly who you are. Can you embrace not knowing this?

Could it be that the mind wants to know for certain what is real and true? It is driven to label it, understand it, to try to narrow it down, and grasp it. (To feel in control of it.)

Could it also be that the spiritual faculties want to release, to expand, and to open wider and wider to Truth? And, that these inherent faculties are completely OK with letting what is Real and True reveal itself to us?

So, instead of developing your ability to figure everything out, what if you developed your capacity to listen to, and receive, Grace? Could it be that all you will ever need to know will be given you when and if you need to know it? And, that even if you don't understand it, Life is somehow governing you and all?

The Meadow Beyond

You are new.   He is new.   She is new.   All is new.
I am new.
There is no old.
See into the new. *Feel* into the new. *Hear* into the new.
The new is always now.

Walk into My meadow.
The meadow beyond the concern for
                              the guilt of yesterday, or
                              the fear of tomorrow.
The space is provided.

Every relationship only exists in My meadow.
Sit still, and walk with Me...
Listen to Me here.
Be the manger.
You will find Me
beyond your well worn paths of delusive reasoning,
        beyond your cleanly pruned hedges of intellectualism,
            beyond your barren islands of absolutism,
                beyond your floods of drowning emotion.

In My meadow, you are invited to
consider the lily in you,
in each, in all.

I am *heard* in the growing tip of the bud.
I am *seen* in the voice of the turtle.
I am *felt* beyond what the senses can reach,
in the ever-revealing Life-force.

I am new. You will find Us there.
In the meadow beyond...

Reality is Good.

Everything that enters your experience is there to reinforce that conclusion.

If something feels peaceful, then you can give thanks for Good. If it feels stressful, or involves suffering, then you can still give immediate thanks because you can see it as a lie to be unlearned, and therefore it turns you back to the truth.

You are equipped with this divine capacity: to celebrate everything.

This is supported by one of my favorite Bible verses: "In every thing give thanks: for this is the will of God...concerning you." (1 Thess. 5:18)

Can you remove the cap from what you believe is possible?

The conditioning of your mind has prescribed limits for everything you do. If you stay solely in your habitual mind, you will be harnessed by conscious and unconscious limitation. This can show up at any time, in any relationship or activity, and is so common you have likely accepted it as "normal."

Spiritual practices can help you access Life beyond the egoic blueprint. They open you to Grace.

So the questions are:
- Are you interested in living beyond the ego?
- If so, what are your preferred spiritual practices that bring you into a direct experience with the Divine?
- How committed are you to these spiritual practices?

Will you answer these questions as if your life depends on it?

(It does.)

Today I asked Grace: "What do I need to see right now?" Here's what I heard:

"I am here. We are One.

"I will reach you no matter what. You can't keep Me away. But, you may not recognize My presence because you have pre-determined how I should show up.

"All I ask is one thing: Never-ending Openness. There are literally infinite possibilities for My angels to break through your mind's crusted mental conditioning and spiritual stereotypes. Where you think you have it figured out, you don't.

"What you get to do is celebrate that your mind has no idea which way I will come to you. So, be receptive to Me coming from literally anywhere and everywhere. This is not a test. It's just that you don't get to call the shots! Your love affair with control needs to be annulled. It is not serving you or anyone.

"I want to make sure you get this, so I will repeat: All I ask is one thing: Never-ending Openness."

(I love it when I get it straight up!)

The separate self is a collection of memories projected into the present and then into the future. From this we have developed what we believe is a concrete view of the world. This perspective may or may not be serving us, since it is based on our conditioned beliefs and memories.

Are you interested in waking up from the dreaming belief of a separate finite self, to an awareness of your unconditioned oneness with all being in Life?

One way to crack open your current worldview is to take things you think you know to be true, and suspend them. Adopt a mindset that your convictions about things are one of many possibilities, but not "the way it is." This could be applied to that which you have read, saw, heard, understood, felt, and experienced.

Start by noticing how much your mind wants to figure it all out so it feels secure in knowing how things work, how you fit in, where you add value, and where you are going. Hit the pause button, and open yourself to a field of awareness beyond what you now understand and know: even one that is outside your current logic.

This is the mindset adopted by quantum physicists, scientists, spiritual sages, and prophets. It allows them to be open to new discoveries. They begin with the mindset that their current view is not reality, but today's best guess, and that there is an infinite amount to unlearn and discover. They see themselves as explorers open to a vast ever-unfolding universe.

When you bring this humble openness to quiet reflective times, as well as your relationships and conversations, you find new, exhilarating and expansive spaces emerging. You learn to celebrate surprises, as you rely on the revelation of Grace.

The vast majority of our education has not been in training to open to grace through surrendering to the Unknown. We are neophytes in this area. Rather, it has been to access knowledge through memorization, analyzing and comparing the known. Even our spiritual practices can become repetitive and stolid.

There is hardened resistance to disturbing our sense of comfort. The mind likes to stay moored in the harbor where it has a minimum of variables and feels securely in control. In this way we are deeply conditioned to avoid transformation and spiritual awakening.

What is the cost of this avoidance?

In your spiritual pursuits, what if you used your mind as a diving board instead of a car you drove around in but never got out of?

Your favorite "go to" spiritual concepts you carry around with you can only take you to where you have already been. Transformation and healing occur through awakening to where you have never been. You have never been in the moment that is unfolding right now. It is Life forever happening in this way for the first time: ever fresh, ever ripe, ready to harvest.

So, let's make the dive and take the leap, beyond what we think we know, what we can see, what we have figured out, what we have memorized, even if we like the ride we are on, and listen, and watch, and feel into this unknown adventure of pure Love.

You may find you have wings that could not be unfurled in your car!

Are you available to Grace? Are you open to receiving Grace? What if being open meant taking what you know is true, and accepting that it is only a miniscule fraction of what is possible to know? When you were a child, this came naturally. Can you find that naturalness again?

Many of us spend our days either trying to convince ourselves that what we know is the complete truth, trying to convince others what we know is right, trying to predict what will happen next, and/or getting disappointed when what we know, or expect, does not happen. This is all part of the ego's attempt to control its world so it feels safe and secure. This is not opening to Grace.

When we have total trust in Truth, then we don't try to sustain anything. What's the point? Truth has it covered. We can let everything go, including the need to figure everything out. We can confidently and joyfully rest in the ever-unfolding moment that is Life. We can open to Grace.

Can you cultivate the humility that is natural to the child in you? This precious child lives in the presence of Grace.

Picture the tip of a pen. Around it visualize the infinite immensity of space in all directions.

Most of us live our lives trying to figure out our options as if they all existed on the pen tip. If we consider life outside the tip, it feels like such an edge that we are afraid to ponder it. We don't trust what we can't grasp.

We are equipped with the apparatus to explore infinity, but not through the conditioning our minds have received from school and society. The head just keeps searching, analyzing, and calculating, asking why things are as they are, and how to fix them. It is tied to the logic within the known.

The intelligence of the heart is better furnished for exploration and transformation. It intuitively feels its deep yearning, which can never be fulfilled within limits, conditions, and creeds. The planet is burgeoning in this moment in the heart space.

I know it is scary, but when you surrender to your heart, your head will follow. (And your life will soar!)

Every spiritual teacher I have read or experienced emphasizes that being completely open is vital to spiritual awakening, transformation, and healing. Over the next five Insights I will offer some "opening exercises" that invite you to go beyond the known. Will you try them with me?

Opening Exercise #1

What if you took
your favorite words
that described
God and man and the universe,
and rode them like a plane
to a recognizable high,
and then leaped out of the plane
into the Unknown,
completely unguarded,
into an experience
where you did not catch yourself
in the familiar?

See what it is like
to stay in free-fall
for an entire minute,
before you pull
your safety chute.

Opening Exercise #2

Think about some world issue that you feel very strongly about. Picture that you are face-to-face with someone who holds the opposite view. Feel what happens inside you as they let you know how completely wrong you are."

Today's open leap into the Unknown:
Let yourself become aware of their perspective as if they are offering you an exquisite orchid they had grown. What a gift! How very kind of them, to share with you something so meaningful to them.

Allow your thought to rest on them and their words without the slightest need to change anything (you wouldn't try to change the orchid). Just notice with curiosity each blossoming idea in what they are saying and how they are saying it. Feel their beauty being expressed in how much effort they have put into growing this viewpoint.

Feel your heart open and your natural smile emerging as you take in the grace of this perfect moment. There is nothing to defend because you are meeting their gift with awareness, understanding, and gratitude. This moment is not about you. They are giving you a gift!

Opening Exercise #3

Think about a situation or person that brings up fear or anxiety for you. Typically this may be something or someone you have been avoiding.

Today's open leap into the Unknown:
Since our conditioned reaction is to close down or run from fear, or to try to control the situation so that the scariness lessens, what might it look like if you opened to it? Can you stay there and experience the fear fully? Don't block it or do anything to try to get rid of it. Instead, feel it. Even embrace it, as if it was a child crying in pain.

Fear is just a part of your beliefs that is not yet informed by Truth. It is your projection about the future that is causing the stress and anxiety. The idea here is to be willing to go through the fear, vs. fighting it. Find out what is in the eye of the storm.

Many things can happen as you sit with fear without resistance. My experience is that it often loses its punch, because when you stop pushing against it your consciousness momentarily rests, and gives Grace a space to land. Why not give it a try? Are you open? Grace won't leave you stranded.

Opening Exercise #4

Picture a time where you instantly disagreed with someone over a small fact. For example: you both looked up what time your flight leaves next week. You say it's 7:20 and they promptly correct you and say it's 7:50. You can vividly remember reading it and you are positive it said 7:20.

How do you respond to their correction? (I have especially seen this scenario with family members or people who have been together for a long time.)

Today's open leap into the Unknown:
Are you completely open to not being right? Can you handle the situation without trying to prove they are wrong? This is a very subtle one, because a response can pop out of your mouth before you have given it a thought.

How you handle the situation communicates what you value most in the relationship:
- Being right
- An accurate time
- Joining with the person and communicating respect and acceptance

Which of following responses do you think they would rather hear?
"Nope, your wrong. I'm sure it's 7:20." Or,
"Great, sounds like we have an extra half an hour. I thought it said 7:20. I'll check again, to make sure we are good to go."

Not only does this kind of an open, gentle, joining response obviate the "who's right?" scenario, it is also a gift to any one else witnessing the interaction.

Opening Exercise #5

It's as if each of us feel stuck watching one TV channel. Our entire view of each other, our world, and ourselves is on this channel. We may be tired of watching a lot of re-runs. We may feel like we are caught in a never-ending soap opera. We may go through very dramatic highs and lows. But, it is all happening on our one channel. And, we are conditioned to believe that this is the only option, the only reality.

Today's open leap into the Unknown:
There is another channel that you can tune into and have an entirely different experience. This other channel is happening in the exact same space and time as your channel. It is just at a different frequency.

On this channel everything is much clearer: the equivalent of high definition and 3-D. This channel is from a network that is designed, produced, and delivered by Grace. It chooses all the programing for you. And you have perfect, free, uninterrupted reception to this channel.

What to do? Commit as your top priority, unlearning and disengaging the frequency of duality, and turning your receptive heart to the reality and frequency of Oneness.

You can't go forward by relying on what you know. You can only awaken by relying on what you don't know.

Memory won't help you awaken. Revelation will!

When you have had a lot of experiences, and you think you know quite a bit, you tend to rely on yourself and what you know. You develop what might be called self-confidence.

When you have had a lot of experiences, and you become convinced you don't really know anything of significance, you rely on and trust Grace. You develop what might be called Grace-confidence.

We are open. Existence is open. Nature is open. God is open. Naturally open. If you doubt this, just put the word "closed" in place of "open" for the first five sentences. It just doesn't feel right. It's unnatural.

Everything exists in and as Consciousness. Ideas are free and always available. Truth is equally accessible to everyone. No one is finitely superior or inferior, for any reason. No one has the inside, walled-off, track to Truth.

The conditioned, human mind does not get this. Instead of opening to the ever-present field of infinite Intelligence, it thinks it needs to close down on, and grasp, a finite set of beliefs and possessions, and build it's life around it. It is always looking for certainty, closure, and a fixed identity.

It wants to feel secure and does what it can to try (in vain) to control its environment. To the degree it is successful it may feel a temporary peace. But, because it is ever-concerned about losing what it has gained, it is always on the defensive: at all times guarding its borders to try to contain the variables that might disrupt it.

Because self-preservation is a defining condition of the human mind, you see it showing up in our personalities, and thus our relationships, organizations, movements, religions, governments, nationalities, etc.

This is one reason openness is so vital. It joins vs. separates. It finds the common ground to "agree with thine adversaries," fostering reconciliation. It shifts the mental model from a competitive "other" and "many," to a cooperative One. It accesses the revelation of Love.

Openness is not just a hopeful choice. It describes our unconditioned essence.

Acknowledgements

So many of you over the past few years have encouraged me to "put these insights in a book!" Thank you to each of you.

This book would have not been possible without Christa Kreutz. She has welcomed this project with open arms and shared her creative expertise and gentle spirit as the editor, graphic artist, and the sole person responsible for the layout. Thank you not only for all you have done, but also for how you have done it. I have felt Grace guiding you all the years I have known you and am so grateful that we have been brought together on this offering of love.

I receive special assistance in helping me send out the Unlearning Insights and post them on Facebook, each evening. I have so much gratitude for Jonathan Hosmer, our behind the scenes website and technology wizard. He is a gentle gift giver in all he does, and his spirit and capabilities have blessed Educare, our friends, and me.

Educare has a small and mighty group of friends that have inspired its development, and volunteer their time and love to support its programs and offerings. They each bless me daily with their Grace-driven lives. Thank you to:
- Heather Barron: a sacred poem of deep and humble compassion, support and wisdom.
- Michael Booth: a silent night of humble, courageous, resilient, authentic love.
- Aileen Cheatham: an ever-awakening presence, whose forgiving eyes and heart continually inspire and bless.
- Dean Furbush: a constant seer beyond ego, straight into the heart of each and all.

- Scott Jenkins: a presence in the wind of Truth, so clear and strong and always there.
- David Littell: a beloved, waking light of humility, courage, and never-ending creativity and love.
- Pierre Pradervand: a silent blessing whose life and words ring with clarity, joy and selfless love.
- Travis Thomas: a living, laughing Yes of pure joy and dedication to transformation!
- Janessa Gans Wilder: a morning star of radiant receptivity, courage, vision and love.

And, I am so deeply grateful for my amazing family whose relentless support is felt and so appreciated daily!
- Annie: my wife, whose patience, love and passion for growth is a light dancing on water: sparkling with resilience, forgiveness and adventure.
- Doug: an ecstatic lens of vision, depth, commitment, creativity and spunk!
- Duncan: an unlimited rhythm of pure trust, deep listening and ceaseless joy!
- Holly: who is moving with the wind of pure inspiration in all she does, blessing us all as she let's Grace dance her forward.
- Laurie: a being tree with clapping leaves of joy, resilience, receptivity and spontaneous creativity!
- Katharine: whose quiet radiance, spirit of adventure and deep love are always there.
- Nancy: my Mom, whose resilience, joie de vivre, generosity, and endless love support us all!

As I deeply feel my gratitude for each of you, and acknowledge Grace as the Source of every idea in this book, a quiet lightening glows within me.

Educare Unlearning Institute

Educare Unlearning Institute offers programs, retreats, vision quests, fireside chats, individual coaching, and a dynamic supportive community for you if you would like to:

- Live freely and authentically from your deepest truth
- Release and nourish new levels of peace, joy, and fulfillment
- Question stressful thoughts and beliefs, and experience transformation through unlearning
- Learn to listen to Grace and each other in a way that naturally enriches relationships and encourages authenticity

You are invited to join us as we create a circle of trust in our small groups. In our space together we use an unlearning process to help you become aware of that which interferes with your ability to live from the innate freedom of Oneness and wholeness.

Unlearning helps you let go of beliefs, concepts, opinions and stories that create limiting self-images, views of others, and worldviews. As you unlearn, or allow Grace to surface and release whatever reinforces your belief in separation, Truth naturally shines forth in radiant brightness, clarity, freedom and love.

Educare Unlearning Institute Programs and Services
You can find out more about our programs and services at:
www.EducareUnlearning.com

Unlearning Insights and Poems
Would you like to receive an original daily Unlearning Insight or poem in your email? Go to: **www.UnlearningInsights.com**
They are also posted daily on Facebook.